FUNDAMENTALS OF MARKETING THE PRIVATE PSYCHOTHERAPY PRACTICE

About the Authors

Bruce D. Forman (Ph.D., Duke University) is Associate Professor in the Counseling Psychology Program, Department of Educational & Psychological Studies, University of Miami. He holds appointments in the Departments of Psychiatry and Family Medicine in the University of Miami School of Medicine and maintains an active private practice.

Kadette S. Forman (M.B.A., University of South Dakota) is a commercial real estate financial analyst for the Courtelis Company in Miami. She is also working on a doctorate in business administration.

FUNDAMENTALS OF MARKETING THE PRIVATE PSYCHOTHERAPY PRACTICE

By

BRUCE D. FORMAN, PH.D.

University of Miami

and

KADETTE S. FORMAN, M.B.A.

Courtelis Company

CHARLES C THOMAS • PUBLISHER
Springfield • Illinois • U.S.A.

Published and Distributed Throughout the World by

CHARLES C THOMAS • PUBLISHER
2600 South First Street
Springfield, Illinois 62794-9265

© *1987 by* CHARLES C THOMAS • PUBLISHER

ISBN 0-398-05299-9

Library of Congress Catalog Card Number: 86-23045

With THOMAS BOOKS *careful attention is given to all details of manufacturing and design. It is the Publisher's desire to present books that are satisfactory as to their physical qualities and artistic possibilities and appropriate for their particular use.* THOMAS BOOKS *will be true to those laws of quality that assure a good name and good will.*

Printed in the United States of America
Q-R-3

Library of Congress Cataloging in Publication Data

Forman, Bruce D.
  Fundamentals of marketing the private psychotherapy
practice.

  Bibliography: p.
  Includes index.
  1. Psychotherapy — Marketing. 2. Psychotherapy —
Practice — Economic aspects. I. Forman, Kadette S.
II. Title
RC455.2.P73F67 1987   616.89'14'0688   86-23045
ISBN 0-398-05299-9

We dedicate this book to our parents . . .
Samuel & Shirley Forman
and
Zachariah (1917-1986) & Mary Stroman

PREFACE

THE COMPLEXION OF private psychotherapy practice has changed dramatically in the past few years. Once it was relatively easy to establish a practice as there was a modest supply of therapists. Now in most geographic areas the ranks of psychotherapists have swelled. Opportunities for employment in governmental and educational settings are limited so therapists have turned to the private sector to earn their livings. What was once an affordable service is now out of the reach of many consumers, particularly if they have no insurance coverage. To survive, therapists are turning more and more to the discipline of marketing. Yet, marketing has been misunderstood by most therapists and maligned by a minority. We are nearing a point in time when basic marketing skills will become a survival tool for all therapists engaged in private practice.

We've talked with dozens of practicing psychotherapists — psychologists, psychiatrists, social workers, counselors — while preparing this book. Many have an intuitive understanding of some aspects of marketing. Virtually none have a clear conception of marketing as a discipline. What little about marketing is known, or used, typically involves selling or advertising — two components of marketing. Our goal is to provide an introduction to the field of marketing as it applies to the private psychotherapy practice. We want to give the reader an overview of the essential elements with a discussion of relevant issues for therapists. We've also included a number of promotional samples obtained from therapists. Since our purpose is educational we've elected to focus on the basic processes. We believe the material is suitable to those just beginning their practices as well as experienced therapists wanting to expand, change the direction of their practice, or who have realized how the business environment is affecting their practice and want to respond accordingly.

In talking to groups of therapists at workshops we've conducted it has become evident, by and large, that therapists have little understanding of marketing fundamentals but want quick advice on how to increase their practice or "market" themselves to one group or another. With an understanding of the marketing basics we outline in this book, therapists should be able to easily diagnose their practice problems and develop a workable solution. Thus, our presentation may be a little heavy on the theoretical side but we agree with the often quoted dictum "there is nothing as practical as a good theory."

We want to extend our thanks to the many therapists we talked with and those who were formally interviewed about their work and their ideas. We also wish to acknowledge the contributions of all who provided samples of brochures, advertising, columns, and so on. Many fine examples could not be included in this volume due to space and other limitations. Appreciation is also expressed to all of our colleagues and graduate students for their support and thoughtful comments.

CONTENTS

FUNDAMENTALS OF MARKETING THE PRIVATE PSYCHOTHERAPY PRACTICE

CHAPTER 1

INTRODUCTION

For MANY READERS of this book the topic of marketing is new and reading this is your introduction to the field. Other readers have had some exposure to marketing concepts and may have used advertising, one aspect of marketing, for building your practices. Yet the field of marketing should not be completely alien to you because as you'll discover, marketing is a part of our everyday lives. Not merely as the consumers of goods and services, but in your professional practice as well only you have not been aware of your marketing activities. Since you haven't had the benefit of a conceptual framework for understanding marketing you may not have understood your actions in terms of marketing and you did not couch them in the vernacular of marketing.

We'd like to begin by inviting you to consider broad categories for understanding the marketing of a private psychotherapy practice. In our view there are four ways to classify approaches to marketing that can be used by a therapist, or any other professional practitioner. The first approach is **No Marketing,** which is merely an ideal. Consider the example of a person who completes graduate training in a mental health field and hopes to immediately fulfill a lifelong dream of opening his own private practice. With the help of his parents, he furnishes and equips an office and puts his name and degree on the door. If one were to pose the question to him, "Are you doing any marketing?" he might say "no." In reality the no marketing approach cannot exist because marketing is a kind of communication and we know that one can **not** not communicate (Watzlawick, Beavin, & Jackson, 1977). By simply placing his name on the door this therapist was engaging in marketing because he was communicating with anyone who happened by that behind the door is a psychotherapist ready to render his services.

Some therapists we interviewed believed they were using no marketing for their practice promotion when actually they employed several marketing techniques. For instance, a psychologist decided to relocate her office to a building where there was more parking space available for her clients. In marketing terms, this relocation of her office was actually a modification of the "place" service feature which provided her clients with easier access to service.

As you'll see later such tactics can be understood as marketing techniques. Practitioners who use these techniques are using the approach we call **Passive Marketing.** This approach is probably the most frequently used by therapists and is based on a lack of familiarity with marketing theory more than anything else. Take the example of P. S., a clinical social worker who worked at a family service agency for seven years before deciding to enter private practice. Over the years she'd gotten to know many physicians, judges, and school teachers through her agency work. Rather than resign her job and devote all of her time to private work, she thought it best to drop down to part time work at her agency and hope that her practice would grow. Soon, professionals she came into contact with through her agency expressed concern that she was not around as much as usual and that her hours for appointments were so limited. She confessed that she was now dividing her time between the agency and private practice. Eventually her practice grew through referrals from contacts she'd made over the years and she was finally able to resign her job at the agency.

Some therapists have moderate familiarity with marketing and very much want to promote their practices. They place ads in the local newspaper and/or telephone directory, and participate in local community groups hoping to attract clients. We call this approach **Intentional Marketing** because the motivation to generate more business is clearly evident. One who used this method was C. J. who completed his psychiatric residency and took a job at a mental health center. C. J. didn't find his work stimulating enough to suit him so he decided to look for greener pastures in private practice. "But where will I get patients?" he asked himself, since he knew he'd have to promote himself in order to generate sufficient referrals to support a practice. He chose to make himself known to the medical community by participating in his city and county medical societies. He volunteered for committee assignments and gave talks on psychotropic medications. In time he was called for consultations and ultimately had a large enough referral base that he was asked to join a growing group practice.

Finally, there is the **Action Marketing** approach which is based on a systematic analysis of practice goals, the environment, consumer behavior, and marketing theory integrated into a consistent plan. To flourish, and not simply survive, in an increasingly competitive field the psychotherapist in private practice must orient her/himself to the business aspects of the practice in a systematic way. That's why we believe the action marketing approach will become ever more important and is advocated in this book. Let's consider A. S., a psychologist who treated his practice like the business he knew it to be. He moved from one part of the country to a location that had several characteristics he thought important: growing population, high income, insufficient number of private mental health service providers. He carefully selected an office location with appeal to potential clients and furnished it accordingly. With the aid of an experienced marketing consultant, A. S. placed ads in local newspapers, magazines, and radio stations. He also wrote news articles and gave free talks to interested groups. Within a few months he had a thriving practice.

Contrary to what some people believe, marketing strategies will never make an inferior good or service become successful among consumers. If anything, marketing techniques will bring the defects into clearer focus, hastening the time of its demise. One very successful therapist who thought quite highly of his clinical skills whom we spoke with said he wished there were more marketing efforts and advertising by psychotherapists. Then, "the lousy ones would go broke and people like me would have more business than we could handle." Obviously he believes consumers are the ones who benefit most from marketing by therapists. Consumers benefit from marketing because as a result they know precisely what they are purchasing, from what kind of provider, and at what cost. This benefit can only occur when there is a free flow of information through marketing efforts to the consumer about the service. Implementation of marketing efforts is necessary to compete successfully in the economic organization of free enterprise.

A fundamental assumption of the free enterprise system is that a society whose individuals are motivated by their own interests will automatically arrange itself for the greatest common good of all its members. This is not a new idea. It was suggested by Adam Smith in *The Wealth of Nations,* in 1776. In this system consumers have the freedom to use their incomes as they wish. To influence consumer choice those with goods or services, such as psychotherapists, must communicate with potential consumers through organized marketing activities.

The U.S. system of business depends largely on the market forces of supply and demand operating in an arena relatively unencumbered by restrictions. Naturally there are government regulations which are imposed upon some activities and these may help at times and other times may hinder free trade. Laws which promote the free flow of commerce; the antitrust laws, for example, are concerned with increasing competition, i.e., aiding consumers. Restrictions which can work against free enterprise are ones like those establishing import quotas on some goods. In 1984, national news media reported the salaries and bonuses the United States automakers were giving their executives. These enormous salaries and bonuses raised the indignation of the American public and government officials. As a result the so-called "voluntary" import quotas on foreign automobiles was questioned. In this situation the less efficient and therefore more expensive automobiles produced domestically were allowed to remain in the market place while cheaper foreign automobiles were limited. In 1980, the last year before the imposition of import quotas by the U.S., Japanese auto manufacturers grossed approximately $4 billion in sales. By 1984 the gross had increased threefold, with only about $1 billion attributable to inflation. How did this happen? Easy. Models with higher prices and loaded with options replaced cheaper—lower profit margin—models so that final sales prices increased. In this way U.S. manufacturers lost the incentive to be cost conscious or competitive and the price of domestic models likewise grew. The bottom line is that this regulatory action resulted in benefits to U.S. automobile manufacturers at the expense of the consumer.

The arena for the free enterprise system is the market place, which may be defined as any place where buyers and sellers come together for the purpose of exchange. Markets organize themselves in a variety of ways. Two forms of market organization that are of interest here are **monopolistic competition** and **oligopolistic competition.**

The market organization of the psychotherapy industry can be depicted primarily as one of monopolistic competition. This is not the same as a monopoly, where one firm dominates the market because there is no substitute for the good or service being offered and competition is virtually nonexistent. Rather, the competitive environment is characterized by many service providers who offer essentially the same service—psychotherapy. One form of psychotherapy can easily be substituted for another. Entry into the profession is restricted so that rules governing who may offer services are strictly enforced. The process of psychotherapy may take the form of psychoanalysis, behavior therapy,

Neuro-linguistic programming, or a host of others. The process distinguishes one school of therapy from another, but no one therapist dominates the market. In addition, therapists can enter or leave the market place with little or no effect on other therapists.

In a monopolistically competitive market structure "price," a controllable variable, is not used as competitive tool. Instead, non-price competition is employed wherein a therapist would choose to call attention to her/his service as either a new, a short-term, or a specialized form of treatment. Another competitive tool is service differentiation. For example, family therapy can be differentiated from other forms of therapy on the basis of which family members are included in the treatment.

As a rule, most firms in a monopolistically competitive market use advertising. This emphasis on communication between providers and consumers encourages the market to automatically adjust itself by allowing firms to move in when supernormal profits appear and leave when profits are subnormal.

In some regions, psychotherapists act more like they are oligopolistically organized. An oligopolistic market organization exists where there are few service providers. In this form of market organization, as with the monopolistically competitive environment, "price" is not used as a competitive tool. Instead, everyone acts together. When one therapist raises fees the others follow. As such, in industries where this market organization exists governmental agencies often suspect collusion. This has not occurred in the psychotherapy business as yet.

The psychotherapist is a person with specialized skills, training, and knowledge. As a group, psychotherapists are unique because their motivations to enter the profession are typically not based on a desire for personal financial gain. Their main objective from which they obtain gratification is to help others lead more successful lives. Without knowing it and often to their dismay when s/he enters private practice the therapist is stepping into the arena of the market place.

On the other hand, practicing psychotherapy is their livelihood and it is necessary that they are able to earn an adequate living at it. Psychotherapists, like everyone else, have families to support and creditors to pay. Rent for the office, the cost of a secretary or answering service, and the telephone, are just a few. A prominent psychologist in Columbia, SC, reported he was going to have to raise his fees, something he had not done in two years. However, in those two years all his office expenses had increased. Satisfaction of one's creditors is critical and enables the psychotherapist to continue providing services. The majority of the therapists we interviewed were not seeking wealth as an outcome of private practice, but did recognize the need for economic gain in order to reach their altruistic goals.

Unfortunately, few training programs for psychotherapists provide adequate preparation in the business aspects of professional roles. Our purpose is to fill at least part of this gap. Our premise is that increasing every psychotherapist's competitiveness in the market place will benefit the practitioner and the consumer alike. More and better services will be available to the consumer and the practitioner will have a wider range of target markets. Once this issue is addressed, psychotherapists can then set about doing what they want most: improving the human condition, promoting well-being in others, and increasing individual freedom.

The authors take the view that the road to successful practice depends primarily upon professional expertise. Psychotherapists must be highly skilled and proficient in the practice of psychotherapy. The schools of thought or theoretical viewpoints you subscribe to are a matter of personal conviction and choice. From the empirical literature we know that different approaches to therapy can have both positive and negative outcomes. So, each therapist must appeal to her/his own value system to arrive at a personal model of how to help clients effectively in a therapeutic situation. With continuing practice and openness to learning we, as therapists, become more adept in assisting clients to reach therapeutic goals; however we, as therapists, or they, as clients, might define the goals.

The authors also make the assumption that therapeutic expertise is no guarantee of success in private practice. We know of therapists who possessed excellent clinical skills who experienced great difficulty keeping their practices afloat. We also came across therapists whose clinical skills were modest but had extremely successful practices. Why? Because private practice is part of a larger system having more complex forces impacting on success or failure. When we therapists treat a client we like to think that expert therapeutic skills are at work to enable the client to learn, achieve insight, experience personal growth, and so on. We believe that whatever improvement comes about is the result of our ability to establish whatever conditions are needed to create change. We are operating in a relatively closed system wherein the important variables are controlled. This system can be depicted simply as shown in Figure 1.

THERAPIST ⸻▶ CLIENT

Figure 1

Over the past decade or so there's been growing recognition among therapists that forces within a client's social system exert significant influences on behavior and adjustment. Accordingly, many therapists responded by considering marital, family, job, and other social environmental forces when working with clients. At present, the "systems" view is within the mainstream of marital and family therapy, while this position also has enough merit to garner the attention of those with other persuasions (Marmor, 1983). This system is depicted in Figure 2.

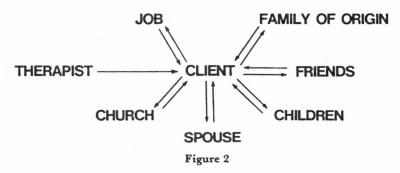

Figure 2

Here, the therapist influences the client's behavior and adjustment but is cognizant of the forces operating on the client via her/his social environment and may include these forces in the intervention strategy.

Since entering private practice places the psychotherapist in the market place, and market forces of supply and demand dictate success more than does professional expertise, we can consider a wide range of forces which operate not only on the client's social environment, but on the therapist's as well. This system may be visualized as shown in Figure 3.

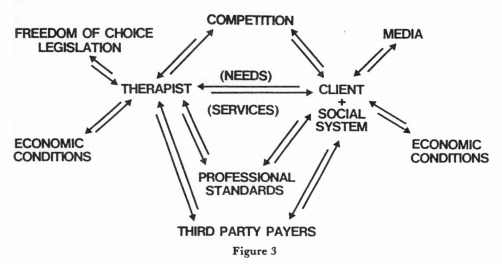

Figure 3

If therapists must operate in the market place it follows that we must understand market forces, particularly those having to do with the practice of psychotherapy. Moreover, we must develop the necessary skills enabling the profession to survive and flourish. In the authors' view the concepts making up the body at knowledge called "marketing" hold promise for success in the market place. Marketing is a tool which can be used by psychotherapists to reach professional goals just as techniques developed in various schools of therapy can be employed to assist clients in solving their problems. It doesn't matter that our orientation might be psychodynamic, if the client has a phobia perhaps we'll use a behavior therapy technique to help the client. Similarly, although we are practicing professionals, and not business people, we can still be pragmatic in our approach to solving our own problems. We need not give up our values as helping professionals when we temporarily don the garb of corporate executives. Instead we simply borrow the tools of their trade as is common practice across professions.

Professional Identification

The profession of psychotherapist is learned by the process of internalizing ideal models with which one comes into contact over an extended period of time. Each of us who has gone through this process of professionalization espouses the values of our discipline. Whether it is psychology, psychiatry, social work, counseling, or marriage and family therapy each acquires a wide range of behaviors and attitudes through the complex mechanisms of the learning process. We learn to conduct interviews, administer tests, prescribe medications, keep case notes, and so on which make up the technical skills that allow us to practice our craft. It's natural for us to want to continue building on these fundamental aspects of our profession through continuing education. In many states, and several professional associations, evidence of continuing education is now mandatory for either licensure or membership renewal. We know that exposure to other viewpoints is a positive experience because it enables a person to develop new insights, which of course promotes psychological growth. What often happens when a person is faced with information which does not fit with he/his usual way of thinking is to reject the entire communication. The person then constructs a set of reason for the rejection which, as they explain, sounds perfectly reasonable. But, if they are unable to leave the new information completely and make an effort to understand it, an interesting phenomenon occurs.

As they begin to shift their menal set they experience emotional discomfort. As you've been suspecting, we're referring to cognitive dissonance. As a person who is also a psychotherapist you already know that you are just as susceptible to this experience as is anyone else.

A profession consists of a shared set of skills, values, and vocabulary obtained by formal training which make it unique as well as distinct from other professions. There is another essential distinction which creates a profession, namely the ability to engage in private practice. If you stop and think about all true professions you'll find this to be a universal characteristic. Accountants, dentists, optometrists, lawyers, and engineers may all be found in their respective private practices. Even teachers practice privately, although on a more limited basis than other professions. While preparing students for their careers the various professions emphasize developing the core skills required to perform at an acceptable competency level. Sometimes trainees are exposed to private practitioners and may even discuss issues related to employment within the private sector. With the exception of psychiatry, few training programs for psychotherapists pay even lip service to the prospect of private practice. Frequently graduate faculty members who have a part-time practice are treated as pariahs, often shunned by other faculty, and given only token raises since they are viewed as making little contribution to the scholarly literature because they do not publish research. Despite the often openly stated aspirations of graduate students for careers in private practice, our training rarely involves exposure to privately practicing therapists or field placements in private practices.

It's easy to understand why so many therapists are anxious about beginning a private practice. Psychotherapy as a privately practiced profession is a business and in many ways is like other businesses. Yet, by virtue of our preparation and identification with professional values we come to believe that being in business is antithetical to practicing psychotherapy. This is unfortunate and is probably more the result of unconscious biases rather than carefully considered judgment.

One of the factors responsible for such biases is that most people's ideas about business come from exposure to manufacturing businesses. Businesses that make and distribute products are more familiar because they deal with tangibles. When we think about business we are reminded of tangible goods that we can touch, use, and consume. Service businesses are concerned with intangibles which makes it necessary to think about their production and distribution somewhat differently.

Rathmell (1974) talks about service businesses having a number of characteristics which distinguish them from product businesses. First, since a service is intangible there can be no transfer of ownership as there is with goods. When you buy gasoline for your car you put it in the tank and use it to run your car. When you have your car washed you receive the benefits of the service but you do not own anything. Similarly, the consumer of a psychotherapist's services does not purchase anything tangible, but receives the benefits of having had the service. These may include having therapeutic results, like insight or behavior change, and may result in memories of a positive relationship with a caring person. However, there is nothing material a client can touch, hold, or give to someone else.

Another feature of service businesses is that the services are sold first, then created and consumed simultaneously. This is quite different from manufactured goods which are first produced and then sold, requiring two distinct operations. Some manufactured goods are sold, then produced, and finally consumed. Construction of new houses can fall into this category.

A third quality of services is their inability to be stockpiled or inventoried. Rathmell makes a case for considering unused services as perishables, since they are subject to fluctuating demand but lack storability.

As compared with manufactured goods, services vary in their quality based on heterogeneity of service provider-service consumer interactions. Since services differ from one situation to the next there is no way to insure that exactly the same service will be performed. This is true also from one service provider to another. An attorney will provide a different service in a divorce case than in one involving a traffic infraction. Similarly, two different attorneys may handle the same case with vastly differing ways and quality.

Finally, a few last points about services which distinguish them from consumer goods is that they cannot be resold through dealers, they are not priced according to a profit over cost formula, and they are not typically consumed by customers but by clients, depositors, patients, passengers, and viewers instead.

CHAPTER SUMMARY

Marketing is part of our everyday lives because we are all consumers of goods and services. Transactions between consumers and producers are the cornerstone of the free enterprise system. Marketing involves a communication between consumers and producers and is thus an integral part of our economy.

There are four categories of marketing activities that can be employed for understanding marketing by therapists. **No marketing** is strictly hypothetical since there cannot be a complete absense of communication. **Passive marketing** is when there is no systematic effort to market. Not because there is no desire, but largely because there is a lack of knowhow. When therapists want to promote their practice and use a few marketing tools, they can be said to use **intentional marketing.** These therapists want to employ marketing techniques but are not going about it in as organized and systematic a manner as they could. When a therapist analyzes practice goals, market opportunities, competitive forces, and consumers, and integrates these data into a plan that is then implemented and evaluated, revised **action marketing** is being used.

The psychotherapy industry may be considered as monopolistically competitive. That is, the market is characterized by a large number of therapists who offer a unitary service which involves service differentiation (i.e., short-term therapy versus psychoanalysis). Requirements for entering the market are highly controlled although occupational barriers are very low. Psychotherapists can enter or leave the market place with little or no effect on other practitioners.

Price is not the main competitive tool in monopolistically competitive market organizations. Instead, service features and differentiation among providers are the main competitive devices.

Becoming successful in a private psychotherapy practice begins with technical expertise. Yet, professional skill is no guarantee of a successful practice. Our position is that in an increasingly competitive market psychotherapists must develop expertise in marketing.

Therapists may have developed biases against marketing because their professional identities as well as through experiences with product marketing. Service businesses differ from product businesses in several ways. The major distinction is that services are intangible. Also, services are sold, then simultaneously produced and consumed. Services can't be stored either. In addition, the quality of a service may vary from one provider to another. Services are not priced according to usual return-on-investment formulas and consumers are rarely referred to as "customers."

REFERENCES

Marmor, J. (1983), Systems thinking in psychiatry: Some theoretical and clinical applications. *American Journal of Psychiatry. 140,* 833-838.

Rathmell, J., (1974), *Marketing in the service sector.* Cambridge, MA: Winthrop.

Watzlawick, P., Beavin, J. & Jackson, D. D., (1967), *Pragmatics of human communication.* New York: Norton.

CHAPTER 2

ORIENTATION TO MARKETING

"My mind's made up — don't try to confuse me with the facts."

— Anon.

FROM TIME TO TIME the above statement or one conveying the same sentiment is heard by most of us. We recognize it as both information overload and sheer opinionation when such messages come from our professional associates. Occasionally it is treated lightly. When we hear these statements from our clients we say "Hmmm, that sounds like resistance." Then we proceed to do whatever is in our chosen therapy model to deal with such behavior.

When it comes to **marketing** this same attitude is evidenced by psychotherapists due to an abundance of misinformation about the subject. We'd like to correct this situation by a discussion of some marketing concepts.

Marketing may be defined as an exchange between a buyer and a seller. More specifically, marketing is the direction of need-satisfying goods or services from producer to consumer (McCarthy, 1981). For psychotherapists, then, marketing is the set of activities which allows the therapist to provide her/his services by anticipating client needs and directing the need-satisfying services to the client. Contained in this definition is what is referred to as the **marketing concept**, wherein the producer directs virtually all efforts to satisfying consumers' needs. That is, providing the service or product the consumer wants. The consumer thus becomes the main focus in the marketing concept. The implementation of this concept is the **marketing orientation**, whose philosphical tenets underlie contemporary marketing practices.

Standing in marked contrast to the marketing orientation is the **production orientation.** Here, most efforts are devoted to producing the

15

good or service to be offered without concern for consumer needs or wants. With a production orientation marketing becomes synonymous with selling because the task becomes one of transferring the product from producers to consumers. It is probably fair to say that a person who is essentially uneducated about marketing theory equates the two concepts. Such a person believes that most businesses subscribe to a production oriented philosophy. This is simply not the case. Despite the fact that the public is exposed to scads of selling, advertising, and public relations efforts, contemporary business eschews a production oriented focus in favor of a marketing oriented one.

The marketing orientation represents an evolution of marketing's function in a firm. Once, marketing was considered just an element of management's activities. It was treated as a set of operations independent of other operations like accounting or inventory control. Eventually, marketing became viewed as more important to a firm's survival. As management's job became increasingly complex and competition grew, emphasis shifted to recognizing the consumer as central to a firm's continued well-being. This shift was assisted by the appearance of Theodore Levitt's, now classic *Harvard Business Review* article, "Marketing Myopia," published in 1960. Levitt persuasively argued that focusing on production rather than consumer needs would likely result in a firm's ultimate demise. Now, managerial thinking has changed so that marketing is considered to serve the firm via linking consumers with all other activities by providing information needed to operate effectively. This way of thinking is **integrated marketing,** a management practice having the marketing concept as a central theme. Integrated marketing is aimed at coordinating all operations so that the objective of having satisfied consumers can be achieved. The tools which management uses are marketing mix, market segmentation, and positioning which we discuss in detail later.

Unfortunately, therapists are not as familiar with the marketing orientation as our colleagues in the business community. There are good reasons for this state of affairs. The production oriented psychotherapist takes the view that the bulk of her/his energies should be devoted to developing and enhancing clinical expertise. Often a decision about what to specialize in is made during one's professional training, or very early in the career. We're encouraged by mentors, teachers, and professional values to do what feels right for us or what fits theoretically into our view of the world. Implicit in this view is that **demand** for whatever kind of therapy is being offered already exists or will grow simply because this or that particular therapy is available. The kind of therapy provided by a production oriented practitioner is offered or "sold" regardless of consumer needs or wants. The production oriented practitioner merely sits in her/his office and waits for the clients to request service. Over time such therapists upgrade their clinical skills (i.e., make technical improvements) so that their services are rendered more efficiently and effectively. Little or no intentional marketing is done by such therapists, although marketing does indeed occur.

A production orientation is also consistent with our professional identities. We take for granted that we must be the most proficient and expert in our therapeutic skills as we possibly can in order to most help our clients. After all, that's what being a psychotherapists is all about. By specializing, it is reasoned, we can concentrate our energies into being excellent in an approach (e.g., psychoanalytically-oriented therapy) or a modality (e.g., sex therapy). Then the specialist believes s/he is able to help virtually any client who shows up for specialized treatment.

This help-rendering value is a noble one. It's engendered by educational and training institutions which are quite adept at transmitting the professional values to the next generation of each discipline. By and large schools and training programs are product oriented. The product offered is in fact a service. Burck (1964) refers to education as "the business of retailing old knowledge and inculcating the habit of acquiring further knowledge." In addition to whatever technical expertise is the substance of training, learners also acquire a particular problem-solving strategy, and with it a view of the world we refer to as professional identity. Few universities make careful empirical studies of the need for trainees of certain disciplines with projections for the future as well as the present. Training programs are often established because of faculty interest or expertise or because of a perceived saleability to potential students. There is little consideration of social, political, or economic conditions affecting future market forces which will determine employment opportunities for graduates. Witness the current glut of masters level mental health practitioners, for example. Over the past two decades dozens of training programs sprang up in universities around the country to fill an immediate desire to offer degrees. For a time students enrolled simply because degrees were available, were available to part-time students, were available at a lower cost, were available with financial aid, and so on since such a degree led to jobs and career enhancement. This was possible because of governmental subsidies to agencies advocated by a society desiring better treatment of its members. Eventually it became evident that there were too many graduates of inferior quality programs and not enough jobs for everyone, particularly in light of declining governmental support for human services. Many of these training programs can be characterized as being of poor quality according to the arbitrary, yet valid, criterion of creating graduates as opposed to emphasizing development of diagnostic, counseling, and applied research skills as do high quality programs. As a result, enrollment fell. The solution? Find ways to recruit students. Lower admission and graduation standards, allow credit for undergraduate coursework as some MSW programs do for students holding BSW degrees, give credit for work experience, or use promotional gimmicks to attract students (e.g., evening or weekend classes; off-campus study like on commuter trains). If successful in bolstering enrollment the program administrator's job is saved, for the time being at least, but s/he must continue with the same kinds of efforts the following semester unless s/he has been granted a promotion for demonstrating administrative talent.

Professional training programs do not have a monopoly on product orientation foci. In the early 1970's our cousin enrolled in a Ph.D. program in mathematics at a prestigious university. During the first gathering of students and faculty the program director was careful to let the students know that getting the coveted Ph.D. even if one excelled, was no guarantee of future employment in the hallowed halls of academe. The old professor said that one must pursue the study of mathematics for love of the subject and not the acquisition of a trade. In many ways we can respect the old professor's frankness for it speaks to the unique place universities hold in our society. Nonetheless, from a marketing standpoint both of the above examples illustrate a definite product orientation. Today, education is very big business. It is unfortunate and expensive for all of us that it is operated with the product oriented focus of a cottage industry.

So, to return to our discussion, we are successful in acquiring the professional values of our respective disciplines in product oriented learning environments supported by institutions equally vigorous in their product orientation. For the most part we psychotherapists do a pretty good job for the public with our professional ethics and valuing of high level clinical skills. But, if we are interested in private practice it behooves the therapist to understand that marketing is an efficient way of connecting her/his services with clients.

A production orientation although it may be well-suited to professional training (not training institutions!) is **not** consistent with the private practice of professional services. Since the production oriented producer focuses effort on production the marketing task becomes selling. Thus, production oriented therapists would be required to sell if they market, so they choose **not** to market at all, because selling just doesn't fit into their view of professional self.

The marketing oriented therapist begins with the consumers. S/he wants to know what consumers want, in what forms they want their services, at what location, when, and at what price. The marketing oriented therapist seeks ways of identifying information about consumers' desires or needs, responds to this information by creating or modifying services, and then promotes the resulting services to that group of consumers for whom the services are specifically intended in ways to which the selected audience is most receptive.

The marketing orientation resembles the therapist's own approach to client care. The psychoanalyst doesn't instruct a mentally retarded person in crisis to lie down on the couch and begin free associating any more than the behavior therapist treats borderline personalities with only relaxation training. We easily recognize either of these circumstances as both ridiculous and unlikely. Yet, both reflect a product orientation. In actual clinical practice we evaluate our clients and determine the most appropriate treatment strategy. This is marketing oriented therapy.

Marketing in Practice

Holding a marketing orientation is a point of view more than an actual set of procedures for carrying out marketing tasks. Once the marketer adopts this perspective s/he is free to use a variety of techniques to achieve the goals of the firm, or in the case of psychotherapists, the **practice.** The authors believe that holding a marketing orientation maximizes the marketer's freedom since s/he is not locked into selling as the major objective. In its ideal form, the marketing concept assumes that if the marketer does a careful and thorough job of accurately assessing demand, and the factors affecting the selected market segment, or what we might think of as potential clients, highly specific and appropriate promotional activities can be conducted. In this way, offensive advertising, merchandising, hype, and hucksterism can be avoided altogether because the firm is directing its efforts towards consumers in the hope of realizing a profit. In short, selling satisfies the needs of the seller; marketing, as Drucker (1973) says, is aimed at making selling superfluous.

To put the marketing concept into practice, start by identifying several essential ingredients in psychotherapy service marketing. These ingredients make up the marketing process.

* IDENTIFY CONSUMER NEEDS
* ANALYZE HOW NEEDS ARE BEING MET
* DECIDE ON FEASIBILITY AND DESIRABILITY OF RESPONDING TO UNMET NEEDS
* DETERMINE POTENTIAL FOR OBTAINING CLIENTS
* IDENTIFY AND SELECT SPECIFIC MARKET SEGMENTS
* DESIGN SERVICES AND SERVICE FEATURES MOST SUITABLE TO SELECTED MARKET SEGMENTS
* DEVELOP A MARKETING PLAN
* IMPLEMENT MARKETING PLAN
* EVALUATE EFFECTIVENESS
* ADJUST AND REDESIGN SERVICES AND MARKETING STRATEGY AS NEEDED

The marketer of psychotherapy, as with any other good or service, carries out the marketing process with consideration of the overall business plan and objectives the firm's management has already formulated. A basic premise of marketing is that the entire process outlined above provides a systematic way of organizing management activities around service to the consumer. Peters and Waterman, in their book *In Search of Excellence* (1982), describe consumer service as one of the distinguishing features of truly successful companies. So we can take a cue from these highly effective and profitable corporations in orienting our practices to serving consumers. The marketing process is data-based and gives you a framework for thinking about how to modify or maintain your pactice. These marketing considerations are not merely tasks you can delegate, like typing and filing, but are germane to top level management's way of working. Like other management functions, marketing assists in achieving broader goals related to the firm's survival and is not an end in itself. A therapist working 45 hours per week who does not want to expand her/his practice but wants to change the focus or to specialize develops a different plan than the one who's goal is to increase the number of billable practice hours.

Before embarking on any marketing at all the psychotherapist must address a question of critical importance:

WILL SOCIETY AS A WHOLE BENEFIT BY LESS INHIBITED MARKETING OF PSYCHOTHERAPISTS' SERVICES?

Obviously the authors believe the answer is an unqualified **yes**, although we don't want to be glib about such an important issue. First, we make the supposition that psychologically mature and emotionally healthy people are desirable in all societies. Further, we assume the more that human beings aspire to these qualities the more each of us benefits since people who are emotionally healthy take more risks, are better able to reach their personal goals, and thereby make life more interesting for the rest of humankind. Secondly, in our view psychologically mature people experience less emotional suffering and are more sensitive to others. As a result they are less likely to intentionally hurt others. Thirdly, we take the position that the services of psychotherapists are a valid way of promoting the welfare of all members of society by promoting personal growth and by reducing emotional suffering. Fourth, because human beings are complex and so are their problems it requires an equally complex and varied body of knowledge to address them. This necessitates the existence of diverse points of view and different specializations of talents. Fifth, it is difficult for people in complex social organizations to have information they require to make informed decisions concerned with acquiring all of the need-satisfying goods and services which allow them to lead full lives. Thus, marketing is of value to society because it is a communication process aimed at linking producers and consumers for the purpose of exchange. The nature of psychotherapy services is often mysterious to potential consumers; communication about its various aspects is more beneficial to members of society than continued ignorance because it enhances consumer choice. The authors believe that marketing is not merely justified. Rather, we see this activity as a social responsibility. Marketing psychotherapy services may not be the task of every therapist, but it is a **duty** of the profession.

The notion of social marketing is not a new concept. It refers to the dissemination of ideas that promote social well-being. Philip Kotler, Howard T. Martin Professor of Marketing at Northwestern University, is generally acknowledged as the founder and spiritual leader of social marketing. Kotler advances the view that marketing is a useless products can also insure that healthful standards are worth adhering to. As psychotherapists, we are concerned with quality of life for ourselves, our clients, and all members of society. Social marketing aimed at improving everyone's quality of life by improving social conditions is a goal of which none of us would take issue.

Quite a bit of use has been made of social marketing strategies for a number of years (Fine, 1981). We've all been exposed to some social marketing but may not have realized at the time what the intent was. For years, a war has been waged against litter, pollution, and environmental destruction. The owl whose motto is "give a hoot, don't pollute" and the Indian with a tear running down his cheek as he observes trash blowing around are part of a series of public service messages. The anti-littering messages are found on television, in magazines, and on bus and subway posters. They are part of an organized effort to promote the **idea** that environmental cleanliness is better than environmental filthiness, and moreover that it is the responsibility of every citizen to assist in achieving this goal. Social consciousness was raised and action was taken and continues to be taken in the sphere of environmental protection.

Most of us can remember the 1974 oil embargo with the fondness of a toothache. As a result of this set of events we now drive 55 MPH—or thereabout—on most U.S. highways. At the time of the embargo a group of people in the federal bureaucracy got together and figured out that people who drove big piggy cars were driving much too fast and gobbling up gas as fast as the Arabs could ship it over to us. If only people could be convinced to slow down there would be plenty of gas for every one and we could all stop wasting our time waiting in lines at the neighborhood service station. Passing legislation wasn't enough. After all people drove above the posted limits already. So a campaign was designed to promote the **idea** that driving slower was everyone's social obligation and would help us get through the gas crunch. Another wrinkle in the campaign was advice on keeping our cars tuned up. That is, if we all don't drive subcompacts the least we can do is keep our gas guzzler operating at maximum efficiency. Then with the sleight of hand a magician uses, they added the notion that slower driving would cause fewer traffic deaths. The result of this social marketing effort is that over a decade later we still have 55 MPH speed limits and have a national fleet of smaller fuel efficient cars.

One of the current social issues is the alarming number of automobile accidents and deaths associated with alcohol abuse. A group of concerned people got together to address this problem in a constructive way.

They began by getting organized into a group called Mothers Against Drunk Drivers (MADD). The group decided to market the **idea** that driving while under the influence of alcohol is bad because people are getting maimed or killed, and those who are responsible for such wanton destruction are not being dealt with in an equitable manner. MADD has been carrying their message to the public. They've given testimony to Congress and influenced legislators to include mandatory jail terms and license revocation in some states. One of the inroads MADD has made is noteworthy because it involves private industry. A brewing company made a decision to put a very low alcohol content beer into production. The company's executives publicly stated they recognize that low alcohol content beer would not solve the social problems associated with drunk driving, but it is a step toward curtailing them. The influence MADD has had with their social marketing campaign on not only the public at large, but on private industry as well underscores the usefulness of marketing to achieve socially beneficial ends.

Social marketing has been used to a limited degree in the mental health arena. Public education campaigns regarding mentally ill persons have been around for a number of years (Ridenour, 1969). These efforts have been the province of public mental health programs, such as NIMH and local mental health authorities, and voluntary associations. Energies have been put into educating members of the public about the prevalence of mental disorders and ways to recognize early signs of emotional trouble. The goals were to lessen the impact of emotional difficulties by early intervention as well as to change attitudes toward people with emotional problems. Other mental health education activities have been aimed at letting the public know about the availability of public mental health facilities. These mental health education efforts have enjoyed varying degrees of success, although many myths remain about mental illness and treatment of emotional problems (Fracchia, et al., 1976). In this regard, there is still much work to be done in the way of consumer education and acceptance of psychotherapy services (Lehman, 1978). Such education can provide a critically important public service by psychotherapists while marketing their own practices.

Many times clients come to their first therapy session with unrealistic expectations. There are clients who believe that therapists are mind readers or experts at solving others' problems (Kupst & Schulman, 1979). Others come in and ask where the couch is or apologize for their inability to remember the dreams they think are expected of them. Then there are the clients who put off going to a therapist completely because they have no accurate information regarding what therapy is about. Instead, they believe only crazy people seek therapy and since they don't perceive themselves as being crazy they needlessly prolong their suffering. There are those who make appeals to other forms of mental health services, such as education **for** mental health which may also be considered a type of marketing tool. These individuals attend time-limited training or workshops on topics that include assertiveness, marital enrichment, and parenting skills, or read self-help books. The authors view workshops and self-help books as important contributions to the mental health field because they've had a significant impact on the lives of many people. These have aided in furthering the public's understanding and awareness of concepts gleaned from the behavioral sciences and make therapy more acceptable to people in need but who otherwise might not seek treatment. Attending workshops or reading self-help books is not, nor should it ever be, a substitute for psychotherapy, in spite of the therapeutic effects that might be obtained from them. Yet, they are of value to psychotherapists because they serve the purpose of marketing the **idea** that therapy is useful and available, as well as giving consumers more accurate information on what psychotherapy and psychotherapists really are. Moreover, changing public views about mental illness and its treatment provides an important contribution to society as well as to advancing the profession. This contribution is social marketing that assists in achieving goals that are in line with most therapist's value systems because it is educational. What's more is that the growth of these tools over the past two decades or so has contributed to the growth of the psychotherapy service industry. We can all be thankful for the advent of human growth workshops and self-help books because they have contributed to increased demand for the psychotherapist's services. Research reports on attitudes toward mentally ill, mental health services, and psychotherapy professions are in accord that more education and accurate information should be provided to the public (e.g., Clark & Martire, 1978; Masserman, 1977). If therapists can help further their own practices while they are contributing to humanity we are also advancing the free enterprise system and validating Adam Smith's dictim that a free market automatically arranges itself for the maximum benefit of all.

CHAPTER SUMMARY

Marketing refers to an exchange between consumers and producers of goods and services wherein the producer seeks to understand the consumer and her/his needs so that goods/services can be designed and produced to meet those specified needs. To elucidate a little further and make this definition more relevant to our own field, we can borrow from Kotler and Connor's (1977) definition of professional service marketing. We can say that marketing psychotherapy services are those activities designed to attract and retain clients by sensing, serving, and satisfying their needs through delivering appropriate services for a fee, in a manner consistent with professional goals and standards.

Subscribing to the marketing concept permits a producer of any good or service to direct activities to consumer satisfaction. A firm that directs its energies to producing and then attempting to sell what it creates is following a production orientation. Such a firm focuses attention on efficient production and assumes its product can be sold simply because it exists.

A firm that focuses its attention on consumers and directs its energies to producing what consumers desire is following a marketing orientation. When a firm subscribes to a marketing orientation and organizes all activities around gathering information from consumers before and after production it is then engaging in integrated marketing.

Society as a whole benefits from the marketing of ideas that improve the quality of life for all of its members. Marketing psychotherapy services is a form of social marketing because the public is educated about mental health, services to assist people with adjustment problems, and where potential consumers can receive the most appropriate services from the therapists who are best suited to meeting particular consumers' needs. The social marketing of psychotherapy provides an essential public service since the notion that therapy services can be useful will promote its acceptance by those in need of this service. Marketing psychotherapy is thus a responsibility of the profession.

CASE EXAMPLE

After 25 years of practice as a psychiatrist and psychoanalytically-oriented psychotherapist, Edmund Cava, M.D. began to notice a change in what he was being asked to do professionally. People wanted more rapid treatment for their complaints. Costs for treatment were getting prohibitively high. Dr. Cava also observed a change in therapeutic technologies. He read a great deal of current literature and after a personal therapeutic experience decided to seek additional training. Then he made a dramatic shift in his approach to treating patients. Instead of long-term insight-oriented treatment he used very brief complaint-focused techniques. "After the first three weeks my office was empty," he exclaimed "because I cured almost all my patients in just a few sessions." Within six months his practice returned to its normal volume and has stayed at an average of 42 hours a week of patient care since 1982. Despite such a busy schedule he looks forward to coming to the office, largely because of the results he obtains for his patients. Because of his success and orientation toward helping patients reach their therapeutic goals Dr. Cava gets an enormous number of referrals; most come from former patients and other psychotherapists. Not surprisingly, Dr. Cava considers himself "incredibly successful."

REFERENCES

Burck, G. (1964), Knowledge: The biggest growth industry of them all. *Fortune, 70,* 128-131.

Clark, R. & Martire, G. (1978), The image of psychiatry today. *Psychiatric Opinion, 15,* 10, 15-16.

Drucker, P. M. (1973) *Management: Tasks, responsibilities, practices.* New York: Harper and Row.

Fine, S. H. (1981), *Marketing ideas and social issues.* New York: Praeger.

Fracchia, J., Canale, D., Cambria E., Ruest, E., & Sheppard, C. (1976), Public views of ex-mental patients: A note on perceived dangerousness and unpredictability. *Psychological Reports, 38,* 495-498.

Kotler, P. (1972), A generic concept of marketing. *Journal of Marketing, 36,* 46-54.

Kotler, P., & Levy, S. J. (1969), Broadening the concept of marketing. *Journal of Marketing, 41,* 71-76.

Kotler, P. & Connor, Jr., R. A. (1977), Marketing professional services. *Journal of Marketing, 41,* 71-76.

Kupst, H. J. & Schulman, J. L. (1969), Comparing professional and lay expectations of psychotherapy. *Psychotherapy: Theory, Research, and Practice, 16,* 237-243.

Lehman, M. K. (1978), Psychiatry in the public eye. *Psychiatric Opinion, 15,* 26-27, 30-31.

Levitt, T. (1960), Marketing myopia. *Harvard Business Review, 59,* 45-56.

Masserman, J. (1977), The travails of psychiatrist. *Current Psychiatric Therapies, 17,* 13-30.

McCarthy, E. Jerome, (1981), *Basic marketing: A managerial approach.* Homewood, IL: Richard D. Irwin.

Peters, T. J. & Waterman, Jr., R. H. (1982), *In search of excellence: Lessons from America's best run companies.* New York: Warner Books.

Ridenour, N. (1969), *Mental health education.* New York: Mental Health Materials Center.

Wilson, A. & West, C. (1981), The marketing of unmentionables. *Harvard Business Review, 57,* 91-102.

CHAPTER 3

PLANNING: A KEY TO SUCCESS

Making a Business Plan

IT WOULD BE unthinkable for most of us to begin therapy with a client and not have a treatment plan of some kind. How would the therapist know where to go? How would s/he know when s/he got a therapeutic outcome? How would the client know when or if treatment was successful? What would we say to the client's insurance company?

When business people set up a firm they establish a business plan with specific objectives. Management establishes the policies and strategies which govern all the activities related to achieving the firm's long-range goals. First they define what is the company's purpose. Do we manufacture widgets or gizmos? Will we also offer curtain cleaning along with our carpet cleaning service? These are questions a firm's management might address when beginning to develop its plan. At the same time management addresses itself to the issue of how the firm relates itself to the larger environment. In other words, management determines the firm's **position** in the market place. That is, it establishes what societal function the firm's goods or services occupies and its relation to other firms pursuing similar goals. Will the widgets be of high quality that only a few can afford or will they be produced for the masses?

Addressing these questions is part of management's responsibilities. A number of years ago managers of large corporations discovered short-sightedness in their planning resulted in trouble for their firms. They became aware of the need to develop long range plans which were both formal and comprehensive. Long range planning assumed that trends from the past could be counted on to continue into the future. Planning then consisted of making projections based on past experiences with only those elements a firm came into contact with during the course of business. The assumption was grounded in a closed system model which

27

has since given way to an open system perspective. Here, the past is viewed as insufficient for making projections regarding costs, market segments, and so forth. Forces outside of the firm in the larger socio-cultural environment are seen as exerting significant influence on the market, and therefore on the firm's activities. Moreover, these forces are in flux, necessitating ongoing assessment and evaluation to take advantage of new opportunities and head off impending catastrophes. Such planning efforts have come to be known as **strategic planning** (Steiner, 1979). Top management in the corporate world recognizes comprehensive planning as an integral part of the managerial function, having ramifications for all of a firm's components and activities. Strategic management is an ongoing process which includes long range plans, medium range plans, and daily or operational plans.

The therapist in private practice must know where s/he is headed to arrive at the desired end state. Planning is an integral part of the management process and as such should be given attention as a tool which can help the therapist achieve her/his practice goals. There are a variety of planning models which can be tapped to assist managers in leading their firms. A specific model need not be used in a dogmatic way, but can be shaped and adapted to meet the uniqueness of both the manager and the firm. What is important, however, is that we, as therapists, develop a perspective on our practices that allows us to function in a flexible manner. Most important is the role of psychotherapist since that is what we do best. Secondly, we are top level managers, or Chief Executive Officers (CEO), because we are responsible for overseeing the entire practice operations. Once we understand our jobs we have a conceptual framework for how to function. Then we can integrate these activities, even though they may seem unrelated.

Planning models have a number of similarities. Each is a set of activities which enables the user to gather relevant data about a firm's operations, make forecasts and predictions, clarify goals, establish goal-directed actions, identify mechanisms for future data collection, and check the results that will be used to correct errors. Most of us have heard of management by objective (MBO) procedures which are commonly used by human service agencies. The MBO system is a "desirability" model specifying what the planner would like to have happen. An alternative approach based on strategic planning is a "feasibility" model which specifies what is possible. The authors prefer the strategic planning approach because it is more comprehesive and emphasizes systems and subsystems of activities. Figure 4, shows an outline of a general strategic planning model that can be useful in getting organized for the future.

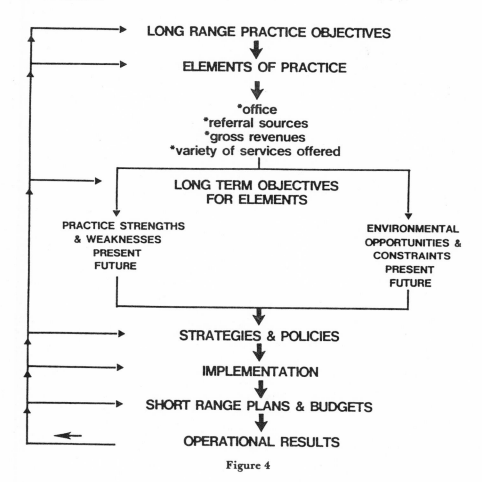

Figure 4

This schema is somewhat abstract and it might be kept in mind as a general model of how the strategic planning process works. It should also be recognized that planning models are useful as a way of thinking about conducting a firm's business which emphasizes evaluating how well the overall strategy for reaching the goals worked. Plans are revised periodically based on performance.

A next step in planning is the business plan. This is a more concrete and specific statement which can be used for either new or existing practices. Figure 5 shows a business plan for a psychotherapist's practice. Jason Petty, MSW has been in practice for five years. He began practicing part-time and three and a half years ago resigned his job to enter full-time practice at age 32. He has a moderately successful practice but perceives himself to be wasting time that he could use to treat clients. He used to covet the free time he spent with his pre-schoolers. Now both children are in school all day and he wants to build up his practice. A business planning form you can use for your own practice is included in this book as Appendix A.

Figure 5

PSYCHOTHERAPY PRACTICE PLAN
FOR JASON PETTY, MSW

I. I offer both short term and long term therapy to children and adults in individual and group sessions. On occasion, I perform custody evaluations for divorce cases. I give talks to parent groups for PTAs, conduct lectures at my church, and have granted interviews to media representatives. I was a member of the Board of Directors at the adolescent residence five years ago.

II. Resources: I rent an office with a small waiting room in an executive building. It's furnished with comfortable chairs, a sofa, a desk, wall hangings, and an area rug, all of which are owned by me. There's enough space for me to meet with up to eight clients.

Finances: My monthly expenses are as follows:

rent (including utilities)	$785
phone	60
insurance (malpractice, health, fire/theft)	135
answering service	40
office supplies; postage	30
secretarial; accounting	100
license/certification renewal fee	40
professional memberships	50
journal subscriptions; books	20
continuing education	175
Monthly Total	$1535

My monthly collections from clients averages $3168. Additionally, $100 per month comes in from an associate who rents my office when I'm not seeing clients.
Expertise: To provide the services I'm currently offering clients I need to have skills in both individual and group therapy. My main strength is in dynamically-oriented intensive treatment. I'd like to improve my skills in treating depression and anxiety

with short-term methods. I'm planning on attending a national conference and a workshop on cognitive and behavior therapies.

Referrals: Most of my clients are referred by other clients who've been treated by me. The next greatest number are self-referred. A psychologist who I send my clients to for testing also refers clients to me. Occasionally I get some clients from clergy and from a pediatrician. I'd like to get more from these sources, as well as attorneys and social service agencies, but have not yet figured out how to do that.

III. Practice Objectives — Long Term Goals: Over the next five years I'd like to have my practice grow so that it grosses $6000-$7000 monthly. In this way I'd keep pretty busy. To do this I need more space which includes a second treatment room that could be rented to two or three part-time therapists who want a furnished office and a source of referrals. I'd want to have a full-time secretary/receptionist and associates with a complementary skills so we could have a wide range of services.

Short Term Goals: Over the next year or so I'd like to increase my volume by 30%. I'm currently conducting an average of 17 sessions a week. I'd like to increase that to 22. If my collection rate stays the same, at 92%, my monthly gross from client fees would jump to $4118. This goal could be accomplished with the same facilities I now have and still be able to take two weeks vacation and spend two weeks on continuing education.

IV. Professional Objectives — Long term: I want to develop a thriving practice and be well-known in my community as an excellent therapist. I'd also like to become a member of the adjunct faculty at the School of Social Work in the neighboring city.

Short Term: I'd like to enhance my skills so that I'm as comfortable and successful in using briefer intervention methods as I am with intensive therapy.

V. Evaluation: I'll be able to tell if my goals have been reached by looking at my pattern of referrals, practice income, whether I've been appointed to the faculty, and if I've moved to a new and larger office.

In big corporations planning is the job of the highest eschalons of management. In smaller businesses, such as the psychotherapy practice, top management is also responsible for many of the functions usually associated with middle management and even non-management. Strauss (1974) discusses several characteristics of small companies which are of interest here. In small firms the CEO is basically an entrepeneur, most management decisions are made at the top, there is frequent and close contact between workers and management, lines of authority are loosely defined, few explicit policies exist, staff functions are often unclearly defined, and there is little money for hiring staff. These factors are important since they influence the kind of planning system a firm will be able to use.

Whether we like it or not a private practitioner who is self-employed is a manager. S/he runs the practice and must be cognizant of the managerial process. Bower (1966) identifies 14 essential responsibilities that are had by managers of all firms. How these activities are carried out is decided upon by whomever serves as CEO of the firm. For us, not only are we the labor who manufactures the service but we also wear the CEO's hat. In this capacity the practitioner must pay careful attention to the 14 functions and carve out a system that works. As a way of introducing you to these functions we'll briefly present each and give an example of how it might be relevant to your practice. We'll use Jason Petty's practice to illustrate.

1. Setting Objectives. The first task is to define the nature of the practice and its overall purpose or mission. The therapist decides on what clientele are to be seen, what the services will be (i.e., psychotherapy only, consultation to certain groups, forensic evaluations), and other fundamental considerations which will guide the growth and reputation of the practice for many years. In Jason Petty's case, his expertise is primarily intensive therapy. He wants to emphasize his skills as an existential therapist but since he has appraised the needs of his clients, he knows that he cannot use this modality exclusively. He therefore is willing to include briefer therapies within the scope of his practice. He also has skills for conducting family evaluations to be used for making custody recommendations in divorce cases that he is willing to continue making available to clients. He finds conducting custody evaluations is emotionally vexing but feels that they provide a valuable service to the community, as well as to offer him an opportunity to have some diversity in his practice. Teaching social work students will also give him some diversity in addition to contributing to his credibility.

2. Planning Strategy. Next, the therapist sets down her/his notions about how to achieve the long range objectives of the practice. S/he decides on the methods to be used in arriving at outcomes which reflect the stated and implicit mission of the practice. Jason Petty stated his interest in both increasing his referral base and having a large enough staff to support a substantial number of clients. He said he had not yet figured out how to achieve his goal of expansion. As is frequently true for psychotherapists, he suspects that he can accomplish practice expansion through effective work. To some extent this was true in the past when the competition was not as keen as it is now and will be in the future. As we'll see in the section on marketing planning, there are several things that Jason Petty can do to facilitate his expansion.

3. Goal Setting. Decisions are made about what specific short range goals are to be implemented so that the ultimate objectives can be reached. These might be related to establishing a referral base, obtaining a contract, or possibly making arrangements to collect fee payments with credit cards. Jason Petty defined his goals for his pactice as increasing practice volume and reality tested his desire by making sure that his schedule and space permit him to reach his goal.

4. Creating a Philosophy. Every firm has a set of underlying philosophical principles that communicate a message of "here's how things go in this operation." This task is not always formal and is rarely written. The philosophy gets conveyed by all of a firm's employees and bespeaks its values and beliefs about the firm's place in the world and its world view in general. Sometimes we hear about organizational climate; the philosophy of the organization is basically what is meant by this term. How a therapist manages 3 a.m. phone calls from a potentially suicidal client, and the extent to which s/he adjusts fees, reveal some of the therapist's values. We've met some therapists who say they'd be willing to slide their fee to almost nothing (i.e., $5) if the client was in need of treatment and motivated enough to benefit from it. On the other hand, one therapist said he'd only slide his fee, regularly $80, to $65; if the client is concerned about fees or wants treatment during irregular hours, this therapist may suggest another therapist to the client.

5. Developing Policies. Management must devise statements to formalize objectives, goals, and philosophy. In some firms policies are often complex and are put into detailed manuals. For the psychotherapist, policy decisions might be centered on whether or not fees are changed for missed appointments, adjusting client fees, or reimbursement practices. It's becoming more popular for therapists to require clients to pay directly and receive assistance in filing claims for insurance. Several psychiatrists we talked to have found it necessary to switch to this procedure over this past few years. One physician opined that there may be a conspiracy among insurance carriers to control fees since he had several experiences where he filed claims, was barraged with paperwork on a patient, exchanged correspondence for a few months, and ended up receiving a small fraction of his claim.

6. Devising an Organizational Structure. In large firms where many people are employed, management is charged with the task of designing a way of getting all the work done with maximum efficiency. The psychotherapist in solo practice is less concerned with organizing personnel and more involved with posting bills for clients and paying her/his own bills. S/he might carry out this management task by emphasizing who handles billing (e.g., self, spouse, secretary). When he first began to practice, Jason Petty did all the billing and accounting himself.

As his practice increased he found these jobs both burdensome and boring. At least it gave him the chance to learn about these necessary evils of business so that he can attend to them without having to do the dirty work himself. He currently has his billing done by an office management service through his accountant. He hopes to employ a full-time secretary one day as well as have a couple of part-time therapists as associates. He's clearly on his way to having a multi-level structure within the next few years and then he'll have the task of defining how these people work together.

7. Human Resource Functions. All recruiting, selecting, hiring, training, paying, and firing fall into the human resource manager's bailiwick. Management decides if and what kind of staff are required and for what purposes. Therapists make all sorts of human resource management decisions like how much to pay themselves and which particular disability insurance to buy. If a receptionist is hired, the therapist must train this individual to greet people in an appropriate way and perhaps to have new clients complete intake information sheets. In Jason Petty's practice he has a part-time associate to whom he leases office space. Although he'd not hired the associate, Jason did perform a personnel selection procedure. Two other therapists had approached Jason about leasing office space and because he was not comfortable with them no arrangement was made.

8. Establishing Procedures. Procedures refer to the specific actions which implement the policies devised by management. Since therapists in private practice rely on collecting fees to earn their living they must have some routine procedures to follow to bill and collect for their services. Procedures for gathering information at intake, how to use psychological testing, and keeping records on clients are also regularly used and reflect therapist-determined policy. Since Jason Petty has a policy of sliding fees he requires a set of procedures to put the policy in force. He's chosen to use income level and number of household members as the basis for sliding his fee. He's made it a practice to talk with his clients about fees during the first session unless it came up during the initial telephone contact. He has found that most of the clients he works with do not desire to have the fee adjusted but talking with them about the prospect of doing so communicates a warmth and caring that he believes enhances rapport, so he continues this practice routinely.

9. Facility and Materials Management. All businesses have a physical location and most require some kind of materials to carry out the firm's goal. Managerial activities here involve all those connected with the location of the plant or offices, their maintenance, and whatever materials and office supplies are necessary. In addition, therapists occasionally arrange for trash removal, parking lot repairs, fixing leaky faucets, and so on besides making rent or mortgage payments. Jason Petty selected his current location and has plans to move to a larger one. He is fortunate that his rent includes utilities. But he pays for this convenience in a slightly higher rent than he'd otherwise pay. He doesn't have a separate bill for electricity and he doesn't have to check the lavatory to make sure there are enough paper towels. Instead he checks on the materials germane to his practice, by keeping up with appointment cards, intake forms, thank you notes, file folders, business cards, postage stamps, and the like.

10. Securing Capital. In general, management tends to all the financial details associated with start-up costs, credit, expansion, and working funds. Professionals, including therapists, are far less concerned with capital than manufacturing firms because their skills take the place of equipment and raw materials. Costs for continuing education and purchasing new furniture or an office computer, however, fall into this management category. Jason Petty's cash flow is just fine now. When he first started practicing, his practice revenues did not always cover his expenses. He was able to make some purchases for his practice on his credit cards, as he did for personal and family items, so he could just pay a little every month. What made matters difficult for Jason, as for the rest of us, were his one-time start up costs needed right at the beginning when funds are tightest. He was able to finance his furniture through the store where he'd bought it, which helped. In addition, he was able to take a substantial tax write-off the year he put it into service. Now that the practice is generating adequate income because of substantial clients Jason is contemplating buying an office computer. He's a little reluctant because of the expense and his mild computer phobia. When he does decide to make his purchase he'll either finance it through the dealer or get a loan from a bank.

11. Setting Standards. Management decides what is an acceptable level of work performance and quality. Therapists decide how many hours to work per day, how many per week, session length, and so forth. Decisions about criteria for treatment termination and treatment success are part of practice standards. If therapists set standards that cannot be met they must either revise them or develop methods for them to be achieved. Jason Petty currently averages 17 client contacts per week and wants to increase them 30% to 22 per week. He must make sure that he gets this many clients somehow. If he is unable to do so he must then revise the standard.

12. Establishing Management Programs and Operational Plans. A firm's management must decide on all the short-term and immediate goals and the precise ways in which they can be met and by whom, by looking at the big picture, so to speak. This managerial function is what is frequently thought of as "management" by many people because of the mundane activities they encompass. Often the entrepeneur working alone carries out these activities intuitively.

13. Information Management. Management requires information on activities within a firm as well as information on what's going on outside. A variety of facts are useful for such purposes as quality control and paying taxes. Therapists must keep tabs on number of clients treated, regularity of payments, and information needed for filing insurance claims (e.g., DSM III diagnoses). Here's where microcomputers prove themselves invaluable and is the main reason Jason Petty plans to get one.

14. Activating People. Management in large firms have to make sure that employees remain motivated and direct their attention to achieving the firm's objectives and goals in ways that are consistent with the firm's philosophy. Psychotherapists who are working alone have to deal with fewer challenges to undermining their business plans. For example, if s/he has a receptionist the therapist may have to insure that appropriate empathy is conveyed to clients who are upset or in crisis. Or, a therapist may have to make sure that s/he does not undermine her/his own practice plans which have been revised. Take Jason Petty, for instance, with his decision to use brief cognitive and behavioral methods for some clients. He must make sure to do what is in the best interests of his practice and to avoid the temptation to do intensive therapy, as he's been accustomed to do.

The Marketing Plan

Without plans a construction crew would just sit around idly and argue about how best to get started on the building and could end up wasting a lot of time, energy, and money on a structure that might collapse. Plans give direction and provide focus. They indicate how large a structure will be, how many rooms it will have, how many floors, and even specifies the materials to be used. Marketing plans serve much the same purpose for a business as building plans do for the contractor. They are the blueprints to work from in conducting all required marketing related activities. In addition to marketing plans being used in general business industries, they can be applied to service businesses too; although the idea of developing a marketing plan for the therapy practice is relatively novel and formal ones are not yet in widespread use.

A marketing plan is simply a formal statement about the direction a practice will take over a fixed period of time with a built in mechanism to measure success. Developing a formal statement of your plan gives you something concrete to refer back to on a regular basis and keeps you from having to clutter up your memory with the details. When you design a marketing plan you put together all of the elements of your business plan and the information gleaned from analyzing your market so that you can integrate the pieces of information into a workable set of actions to help you achieve the goals you've established for yourself. Plans don't have to be carved in stone so that you get bogged down to the point where you can't do anything that isn't in the plan. In fact, experts in strategic planning advise against doing so. This can enable management to take advantage of new opportunities and changing circumstances. Your plan should be flexible and serve you by keeping you on the road to success, preventing problems that are avoidable, and limiting the surprises that often arise. You should be in a better position to periodically revise your activities and goals with a carefully devised plan than without one. Your plan allows you to think ahead and not react in an ad hoc way to daily changes in market conditions, a tactic that can spell disaster in the long run. You can be the architect of your future if you remember that planning is an ongoing process.

Marketing plans contain several features which aid management in outlining the current position, desired end-state, and how to get there. Ideally, the plan contains more than the marketing mix or strategy for advertising (we'll discuss those later). You also need to include the way or ways the plans that are carried out are to be evaluated so that corrective action can be taken when needed. Next, elements of a marketing plan are presented and a suggested format for organizing your plan is offered. Remember, it is more important that you develop a plan that works for you in your particular situation than it is that you follow the format to the letter. There is no one right way to prepare a marketing plan. There are many different plan outlines that have been followed by firms and all seem to be successful in helping those firms meet their goals. If you are interested in taking a closer look at some of the sources we've consulted you can find the bibliographic information in our reference section for Berkowitz and Flexner (1978), Winston (1983), and

Schmeling (1984). Before continuing our discussion we suggest you glance over the example shown as Figure 6. A marketing planning form is included as Appendix B.

Figure 6

MARKETING PLAN FOR JASON PETTY, MSW

I. Mission Statement. My purpose for conducting my practice is to help people in need of psychotherapeutic services to aid them in coping with the fundamental problems of living. The services I offer are short-term and long-term therapy. I treat people of all ages including children, adolescents, and adults. I use individual and group treatment methods. I also perform custody evaluations in divorce cases and give speeches to lay groups.

II. Situation Analysis. My city is located in a central Atlantic state with a population of just under 161,000. Of these, 26.4% are under 18 years of age, 17.6% are between 18 and 24, 16.8% are between 25 and 34, 16.8% are aged 35 to 49, and 22.4% are over 50. The median age is 28.6 years. There are 55,800 households with a median effective buying income of $18,808, or how much money is available for spending. Approximately 24% of households have effective buying incomes of over $25,000, and 33.5% have effective buying incomes of $15,000 to $25,000, compared with only 6% having disposable incomes of less than $10,000 annually.

Using the most recent figures on psychiatric epidemiology, I estimate that at any given point in time roughly 22% of the population will have a diagnosable emotional disorder. This figure does not include transitory adjustment problems like marital distress, and stress-related problems. I can conservatively add 3% to this figure. Thus, for the two highest income groups I estimate there to be 23,143 people in my city who are potential users of a therapist's services. I also know that only around 35% of these individuals will seek care for their troubles but not all from mental health providers.

There is a fairly high concentration of mental health service providers in private practice here because of the moderately high standard of living. There are now 18 psychiatrists, 22 Ph.D. level psychologists, 10 clinical social workers, and 7 marriage and family therapists. In this sector the fees range from $45 to $80 per session. My fees are on the low end of the spectrum compared with all disciplines and are about average compared to other social workers. The position I occupy vis-a-vis other therapists is that I'm one of only a handful that identify themselves as existential. Yet, I'm also viewed as a generalist having specialized skills in intensive therapy, group procedures, child treatment, and custody evaluation.

In addition to private practitioners there is a community mental health center that caters mostly to lower income groups with more severe disorders. So there is little competition. But, there is competition from a church-sponsored social service agency that has been expanded into providing psychotherapy over the past two years; their growth has leveled off recently.

In reviewing my practice characteristics for the past six months, I find that I have an average of 66 client contacts per month. I generally conduct one group therapy session with adults each week, treat four children and 12 adults, and conduct one custody evaluation per month. My base fee is $55 but I occasionally adjust it to $30, so my average is $50, adjusted for the collection rate (92%) it's $46. I charge $20 for 1 ½ hour group session. Since I typically spend two to three hours on a custody evaluation, I charge $110 for this service. Third party payments account for less than 5% of my practice which I think accounts for my high collection rate.

Referrals come from other clients mostly. I also get referrals from other professionals as follows: psychologist = 2/month, clergy = 1/month, physicians = 1/2/month, family court = 1/month. Other referral sources with potential are schools, attorneys, pediatric and OB/GYN specialists.

The stages in my life cycle are

> practice: growth stage
> self: growth stage
> favored treatment mode: mature stage

III. Trend Analysis. The social trends I've noticed in the recent past are the explosion of interest in computer technology, growth of fitness and nutritional pastimes as health consciousness increases, more awareness and willingness to talk about child sexual abuse, and a tapering off of the divorce rate.

From what I've been observing and hearing, people I come into contact with talk about whether I think the next year will witness a stability in economic growth along with discontent. I foresee more people moonlighting and more family members working. I think people are going to be more interested in getting extra money for consumer goods and saving for children's educations and for vacations. I think there will be less enjoyment and more stress, so employers will want to do something helpful for their workers lest productivity suffer.

To prepare for these possible trends I will develop my skills in brief therapy and stress management procedures. I must also learn about exercise and nutrition and their role in managing stress and in emotional well-being plus develop ways of integrating them into my practice.

IV. Problems. Economic problems could enable fewer people to afford therapy out of their own pockets. If this happened in my practice I would consider lowering my fees, make extended payment plans available, integrate alternative payment plans like credit cards, and barter for needed services.

Although there seems to be a surge of interest in health promotion, I don't know much about the field. Although I'm willing to learn, I have other priorities in my practice. Also, my image is one of a mental health provider rather than a health promoter.

Third party payers have been showing increasing reluctance to reimburse for mental health services and wish to make the payments small. Third party payments are not a mainstay of my practice, but if physicians and psychologists continue having trouble collecting, prevailing fees might be lowered so they compete in my market.

V. Marketing Objectives. I want to increase services to individual adults by 20% over the next year and by 30% within five years. I want to continue having about the same amount of long-term therapy clients but want to increase the number of brief treatment cases. I'm interested in treating adults with anxieties and phobias since the most recent NIMH figures suggest these problems have a relatively high incidence. They are also amenable to brief treatment.

The services I plan to offer are brief therapy aimed at anxiety reduction and development of new behavior patterns. There are more females than males with these problems and they tend to be young adults who are not college educated. I believe the problems of anxieties and phobias are not viewed as emotional illnesses by these people, but rather they are considered inconveniences that restrict their lives a bit. I think this makes it easier for non-medical therapist to treat them because they can avoid the illness label.

VI. Marketing Strategy for Each Segment.

A. Pyschotherapy clients.

1. Marketing mix: comfortable office, central location, moderate fees, individual and group treatment available.

2. Promotional tools: personal sales with referral agents and with clients.

3. Goal: obtain more clients through educating referral agents that I want to treat more people.

4. Message: "I can help people cope better; I'm a person who cares."

Anxious/Phobic Clients.

1. Marketing mix: structured groups, specialized services, special fee.

2. Promotional tools: personal sales — with clients and referral agents, sales promotion — by special pricing, advertising — in local paper, publicity — by getting interviewed by local paper.

3. Goals: educate about services; change attitude toward problems of anxieties and phobias; change perception of my therapy skills and interests.

4. Message: "Anxieties and phobias are normal living problems," "They can be treated easily with a minimum of inconvenience and usually without intensive therapy."

VII. Resource Allocation. I will devote two hours per week, on the average, to implementing and overseeing my marketing plan. I'll set aside around 5% of my total practice gross, or $2000, to get my plans in operation. I'll personally be involved in all phases of the plan. I will write the advertising copy and interact with advertising sales reps. Since it's my practice I'm promoting and no one knows better than me what I do, I will do all personal selling with referral agents and my clients.

VIII. Control and Review. I will know that I've successfully marketed my practice when I've increased my client load an additional 30%. I'll know I've been successful with entering into the new segment of anxious/phobic clients when I'm spending time every week treating these clients. Initially this should include one group per week and after six months should include three to five clients weekly. I intend to review my progress monthly and after one year I shall revise my plan.

I. The Mission Statement

When organizations construct a formal marketing plan it often begins with a review of the organization's business objectives outlining the nature of the business and its intentions. This is done so the plan can stand alone and anyone picking it up will be able to get a clear picture of the plan for marketing activities vis-a-vis the overall activities of the firm. You can refer back to your business plan and recapitulate it here. If you've skipped a formal presentation of a business plan you can simply jot down your statement of what you believe your objectives are for your practice. The mission statement provides the foundation for the rest of the plan.

II. Situation Analysis

The next step is for you to consider ways in which your market can be meaningfully segmented, how the segments are currently being served, by whom, at what fees. The purpose is for you to determine what is currently going on in your market and forces that might influence your marketing activities. You will also include your current practice characteristics (e.g., number and type of clients treated, fee structure, referral base, collection rate). Basically you are attempting to realistically assess your current position in the business environment as it actually exists. You are also identifying whether or not new services may be needed and just what they might be, plus your potential for successfully delivering them. It's also important to identify your image or how clients and referral agents view you and your practice in terms of the service features. It can be useful to use quantitative information as well as your impressions and intuition, whenever such data are available. One indicator of image is the kind of referrals you get. You can simply examine your appointment book and categorize your clients into groups that make sense to you. You might discover that you receive certain types of clients with more regularity than other types. You might be able to classify your clients by type of problem, income, religion, or a combination of parameters. You may find it possible to assess your image based on feedback from clients. For instance, a university professor who also has a thriving private practice was treating a young couple at a very reduced rate because they were obviously in dire need and unable to afford his regular fee. Upon learning of the couple's plight, the wife's parents offered financial assistance to the couple to assure that marital counseling could continue. At that point, the couple sought treatment from what they described as a "real therapist" who charged them the full fee. Needless to say, this therapist was much chagrined to discover his image as an "ersatz therapist."

The concept of product life cycle may also be applied here. Since psychotherapy is not a product, but rather a service, it is helpful to think in terms of life cycle of the therapist and life cycle of the intervention modality. In product manufacturing circles an item is viewed as going through four distinct phases: market introduction, growth, maturity, and decline. You can think about your practice and your career as a psychotherapist as going through essentially the same cycle. The therapist who is just beginning will manage her/his practice quite differently than the therapist who is nearing retirement. For example, referral bases can vary significantly during different phases of the life cycle. Jeff Spar, Ph.D., observed that early in his practice referrals came primarily from other professionals but eventually came mostly from those he treated. We've found that most therapists with established practices generally concur with this conclusion.

Robert D. Weitz, Ph.D., who in the early 1940s was one of three clinical psychologists in full-time private practice in the United States now is in semi-retirement. He spends no more than 10 hours a week doing therapy. He could easily fill his appointment book but prefers to serve as Chairman of the Board at Nova University's School of Professional Psychology, edit a professional journal, play tennis, and enjoy himself. Twenty years ago he would have opted to fill his appointment book. Edward J. Carroll, M.D., still practicing at age 76, joked that people not only wonder if he's still seeing patients, but also if he'll live long enough to finish treating them. So in making your situation analysis assess where you currently are in your practice and professional life cycle.

Similarly, models and modalities of therapeutic practice also have life cycles. Psychoanalysis, in our opinion, is in the declining phase. There is still demand for this kind of treatment but the current social and economic climate has created demand for more rapid and cost effective methods of change. Behavior therapy is in the mature stage, while family therapy seems to be in the growth stage. Other modalities, like stress management, neuropsychological assessment, lifestyle counseling, and pain management, can be classified into one of the categories of life cycle too.

III. Trend Analysis

Here you note what kind of trends you've been observing in the field in general and in your market. Perhaps you've noticed more and more in the journals on stress management or the growth of dual career marriages. Naturally if you don't read professional journals or newspapers you won't have much of an idea about current trends. But if you're that kind of person it's probably because your practice is brimming with clients and you're doing a fine marketing job already. It will also be of use to review current trends in your own professional development. Perhaps you've been getting increasingly interested in hypnosis or you've cultivated a interest in divorce counseling. These interests will certainly have a hand in influencing the direction your practice will take, if not a prime motivator. Other people's views concerning social trends can also give you a perspective. One particularly useful resource is Daniel Yankelovich's book, *New Rules,* in which he outlines his notions about changing values and their influence on American lifestyles.

In our example, some trends were identified which appear to be national in scope while others were less sweeping. Here the observation was made that computer technology was growing in interest and application. This is a national or perhaps an international trend, having significant implications for therapists. The therapist in our example has at least paid lip service to the influence of computers by indicating recognition of the trend in his business plan. He has chosen not to do anything about it for the present and therefore excluded it from this year's marketing plan. He's assured us that computer literacy and a purchase both have high priority for next year as he anticipates a growth in his practice which he thinks demands a computer. He is also counting on advanced technology and competition working to his advantage so that he'll be able to get a more sophisticated computer system for less money than he'd have to spend now.

IV. Problems and Opportunities

In this section you identify all the difficulties which could conceivably arise in your efforts to target services to existing segments and to new ones you're considering. Here you'll include any potential risks that may be incurred. These might be risks to your image, your work style, or your financial security among others. At the same time you should consider opportunities that are anticipated based on some tangible evidence. The threats and opportunities you review should be both internal and external to your practice. Some firms also plan for the unexpected by constructing a few scenarios of unexpected yet possible events in the form of "what if . . ." statements so that contingency plans can be made. The best course of action to use with this section is to be extremely honest in your appraisal of your strengths and weaknesses for dealing with whatever you critically determine to be problems and opportunities.

V. Marketing Objectives

Now you are ready to decide on your target segment or segments. You can evaluate the potential for marketing to them and have a reasonable degree of certainty of your chances for successfully doing so. You will decide if you are going to target your efforts to increase services to current clients, to potential clients within the segment you are already serving, some new segment, or a combination of segments. At this point you should have a pretty good idea about the characteristics of your market and should be able to define the essential geographic, demographic, psychographic features along with the number of potential consumers within the segment. The more accurate the information is about your identified segment, the more likely you will be in developing the most suitable promotional strategies to communicate with them.

VI. Marketing Strategy

A variety of strategies exist to achieve marketing goals for manufactured goods which can be readily transferred to service marketing. Clever techniques and gimmicks are well-known to all of us because of exposure to them through media with which we commonly come into contact. We recommend that you consider strategies that fit with your overall marketing and business plans rather than those that seem to be cute or are emotionally appealing to you. The overriding factor in planning strategy is the answer to the question "What strategy will my target segment be the most likely to respond?" To assist in your decision consider some of the strategies listed below.

1. Innovation: Focus on benefits to consumers in ways that are novel or in ways they have not considered; use of a therapist's services for applications where they have been underutilized or are new, such as Employee Assistance Programming. Parke Fitzhugh, Ph.D., used his knowledge of management, hypnosis, and psychology to obtain contracts to work with the Metro Dade Police Department, in Miami. His unique skills gave him the opportunity to conduct training, consultation, and counseling with various components of law enforcement and fire departments. Another innovation is the use of computerized assessments. Grover C. Loughmiller, Ph.D., of Tyler, TX, offers clients the chance to get career testing completely by computer. For some clients this is the first time they ever sat at a keyboard and interacted directly with a computer.

2. Multi-Brand Approach: If we think of particular therapeutic schools as "brands" you can develop an inventory of brands, to make available to clients, by forming a group practice where psychoanalytic, behavioral, and gestalt therapists are available, or you can obtain additional skills for practicing a variety of therapy systems. In our example, Jason Petty who is already skilled in existential therapy plans to add brief problem-focused treatment to his bag of tools to offer his clients.

3. Fortification or Flanking: This is the tactic of having several different sizes of essentially the same product. For a therapist this strategy can involve modifying session length or frequency, or it might be used by making both individual and group treatment available. Alan Schlaks, Ph.D., of Hollywood, FL, offers clients the opportunity to contract for sessions of varying lengths based on 15 minute intervals. He has some clients getting 30 minute sessions, some for 45 minutes, some for 60 minutes.

4. Intensive Advertising or Publicity: This means planning a campaign around a theme, using a variety of methods, perhaps concentrating on one particular medium in an effort to achieve greater visibility. Some practitioners have successfully used newspaper ads, others have conducted public relations campaigns exclusively, while other therapists have focused their energies on distribution of their brochures through referral agents.

5. Aggressive Personal Sales: This is a method a therapist might use to increase referrals from one particular source or group. The therapist who wants to maximize physician referrals by increasing social contact with this group is using an aggressive personal sales strategy. Charles G. Plyler, M. D. routinely visited with other physicians in the surgeons' get-ready room after he completed rounds with his own hospitalized patients. He'd hang around and talk to the surgeons about their work, look at x-rays, and just "talk smart" as he put it, without having responsibility for patient care. He was genuinely interested in medicine and it was apparent to the surgeons. Yet, he claims he knew that these activities, although fun for him, were an important part of his work and crucial to building and maintaining his practice.

6. Premium Pricing: An effort to garner a particular segment by using what amounts to snob appeal or a desire to assure that one is purchasing the best possible quality. Many yuppies, for example, seem to make purchasing decisions based on what might be termed an exclusivity motive. Cars like Mercedes-Benz are bought not so much because they are three times better than cars costing one third of the price as they are bought because so few people can afford to buy the more expensive car. For many years Coca Cola has been able to maintain a strong market position despite intense competition and a comparatively higher price. Psychoanalysis has been the Coca Cola of therapy and has been able to survive because of the widely held belief, particularly among physicians, that it is the prestige form of therapy.

7. Confrontation: The term used when the competition is met head on by price cutting and emphasizing that virtually the same service available elsewhere can be obtained at a price that is below the competition's. This strategy is used in overcrowded markets when the competition is fierce. It is not used much in professional services probably because of the general expectation by consumers that higher fees equate with higher quality.

8. Full-Line: The strategy that consists of having the inventory of skills, techniques, and perhaps staff to provide any client with virtually any therapeutic a need that may arise. Therapists who are generalists and call themselves eclectic are using this strategy. Use of this strategy can be made by having a file full of various tests, biofeedback equipment, training in an array of therapeutic skills, and having easy access to physicians for medication maintenance. Therapists who become part of a Preferred Provider Organization or PPO are making use of this approach.

9. Special Financing: A service feature that may involve such tactics as using a sliding fee scale, negotiating on fees, accepting credit cards, or accepting assignment of third party payers as payment in full. Assuming responsibility for filing claims with third party payers can be part of this strategy, as can bartering for goods or services the client may have. W. Vail Williams, Ph.D., new of Sioux Falls, SD, once treated the son of a farmer in exchange for several pick-up truck loads of firewood. Tony Sabatasso, Ph.D., of Mill Valley, CA barters for his services on an organized basis by offering his services through a barter club.

10. Distribution Innovation: This means that place is modified or promoted. Some therapists use satellite offices, or have various locations available out of which to work. One professor acquaintance uses the modest office space available to him at his university for meeting the needs of a price-conscious segment. Yet, for upper-middle class clients he uses space in a physician's office he sublets that is more lavishly decorated, enabling him to charge a higher fee. Another therapist advertised that he will go to clients' homes to conduct therapy.

11. Specific Consumer Specialization: This refers to focusing on one kind of problem, such as treatment of pain or catering to one category of referral agent, such as relying on orthopedic surgeons for pain management cases. Dennis J. Buchholz, Ph.D., of Louisville, KY was trained as a physiological psychologist. After completing a respecialization program in clinical psychology he became highly skilled in clinical neuropsychology. He is now sought after by neurologists for conducting assessments, particularly for patients who are victims of head trauma.

12. Vertical Service Specialization: This means that the focus is not on one class of problem but on a variety of interventions for a broad class of client needs. Here the therapist might specialize in family therapy or women clients and offer a broad spectrum of services.

13. Job Specialization: This is when a therapist focuses attention on the treatment on one kind of problem, such as obesity, smoking cessation, or treating agoraphobia.

14. Sales Promotion: Employs the strategy of relying on contests, discount coupons, free gifts, premiums (e.g., trading stamps), and so on. The most common promotional tool therapists are using is a first interview or "consultation" without charge. Another is the use of demonstrations of some of the techniques therapists use in their practice. Bruce J. Schell, Ph.D. of Columbia, SC, reports that when he is providing training to various lay and professional groups, he demonstrates the techniques he actually uses in his practice. In this way, he says "the mystery of psychotherapy is resolved." He also reports potential clients and referral agents can then claim they experienced, albeit indirectly, rather than merely heard about thus and such. They are in a position to know the techniques he uses and decide whether or not they want that kind of treatment. This is a useful strategy for overcoming the problem of sampling a service before it is consumed. Many service businesses have the same kind of problem to overcome. Think of how difficult it would be to sample the services of a particular bank without first becoming a customer.

15. Lower Cost: Different than lowering price, since price and cost are not necessarily the same. Lowering price as in the confrontation strategy is based on reducing profit on unit sales which are made up by increasing volume. Lowering costs enable price to be lowered by modifying elements of production cost or the perceived psychological or social costs to the client. This may be a difficult concept for therapists to understand since therapy is a service and it is not possible to compute a production cost on a unit basis. It is possible to calculate the cost of running a practice. So, a therapist who pays careful attention to the basic operation costs and makes an effort to lower them can be said to use a cost lowering strategy. Clearer examples are the therapist who moves her/his practice to an office with lower rent or who employs associates who work under supervision. The therapist who moves the practice to a location more convenient to public transportation, or modifies the waiting area to make it more private is also employing this strategy. Another cost lowering strategy is to use a computerized billing system and post bills yourself on your personal computer.

16. Creating Tangibility: Important for products and even more important for service businesses. Some practitioners have adopted the practice of sending out newsletters to both past and active clients along with potential referral agents. The newsletter includes developments in their skills or professional contributions along with self-help tips and advances in the field that were gleaned from journal articles. Discussing psychological test data with clients during treatment planning sessions also contributes to tangibility.

17. Image Transformation: Aimed at changing perceptions of the practitioner which may be helped by clients or referral agents. The strategy can be carried out using a variety of tactics, having the ultimate goal of modifying how the therapist is perceived. For example, a therapist can work toward being accepted as providing services that are preventative and health promoting, in contrast to treating disturbed individuals. Jack Tapp, Ph.D., practices what he considers a unique approach to holistic health and behavioral medicine. A few years ago he began calling himself a health psychologist and was apparently the first to use this designation. His image is now rather distinctive.

VII. Resource Allocation

The next step is to fix costs for the chosen strategies. There is no set amount of money that should be spent on a marketing program. Some firms, particularly large ones, spend between four to six per cent of their gross income. Ten per cent appears to be the limit that can allow for optimal return on investment. You also should determine who is going to have responsibility for what tasks. If you decide to have brochures printed you can specify which companies you will consider. If you choose to contract with an advertising agency, decide which this will be. If you decide to increase exposure through publicity, state how much time you will spend on these efforts.

VIII. Control and Review

Finally you must decide how and when your marketing program will be monitored. Will you review your activities weekly? monthly? or quarterly? You will also need to develop some way of calculating if your time, energy, and money have the payoff you intended and whether or not the outcome makes your efforts worthwhile.

CHAPTER SUMMARY

"Plans," as General Dwight D. Eisenhower is often quoted as saying "are nothing." But he went on to add "planning is everything." Planning is the job of management which establishes all policies and procedures that are required for a firm to realize its objectives. Activities surrounding planning involve the sustaining elements of an organization because they translate to survival.

As the CEO of your practice you must understand the multifaceted responsibilties of this office. You are in the unique position of being both management and labor. To be successful you must plan and implement a managerial system that works. You are already skilled in performing the job of psychotherapist. In the private practice business you, as manager, are required to master the roles of management and simultaneously juggle them while still wearing the hat of therapist. The CEO sets overall objectives, plans strategies, decides on short-range goals, creates a philosophy, articulates policies, establishes procedures, defines organizational structure, manages and motivates personnel, manages the physical facilities, secures capital, sets standards, and manages information.

There are many planning models in existence that can be useful for constructing a business plan. Strategic planning models are viewed as useful approaches because they incorporate what is actually possible as opposed to what is desirable. A strategic planning format is comprehensive and gives managers the opportunity to focus on systems and subsystems of activities.

After a business plan is completed a marketing plan can be devised. Marketing planning is an integral part of overall management. It is not an activity that should be delegated to those who are not involved in high level management. Instead it is a prerogitive of the highest level decision makers.

Marketing plans provide the therapist with the mechanism through which her/his planning efforts are carried out over a fixed period of time. Plans have the additional features of outlining the current position the practitioner occupies in relation to other therapists and specifying what steps are needed to reach one's goals. Finally, they give the therapist the chance to establish parameters by which s/he will judge success.

While useful for carrying out the inherently valuable planning process therapists are cautioned against treating the resulting plan as something with a life all its own. Remember, it's the **planning** that's important, not the plan.

REFERENCES

Berkowitz, E. N. & Flexner, W. A., (1978), The marketing audit: A tool for health service organizations. *Health Care Management Review, 3* (4), 51-57.

Bower, M. (1966) *The will to manage: Corporate success through programmed management.* New York: McGraw-Hill.

Schmeling, D. G. (1984), Developing a mental health marketing plan: Ten surefire steps to success. *Health Marketing Quarterly,* (1), 5-11.

Steiner, G. A. (1974), *Strategic planning.* New York: Free Press.

Strauss, G. (1974), Adolescence in organizational growth: Problems, pains, possibilities. *Organizational Dynamics, Spring,* 2-17.

Winston, W. J. (1983), Marketing planning for group practices. *Health Marketing Quarterly, 1* (1), 13-22.

Yankelovich, D. (1981), *New Rules: Searching for self fulfillment in a world turned upside down.* New York: Random House.

CHAPTER 4

THE MARKET ANALYSIS

A N ADVANTAGE OF the free enterprise system is that virtually any producer who wishes to enter the market place to offer a good or service is free to do so. Throughout history many individuals and firms have done just that. Some have been successful while others have failed miserably. Success or failure depends primarily on a thorough understanding of the interaction of the market forces. For any firm to succeed in the market place the market forces of supply and demand must be appropriately addressed.

Each product and service has its own demand state in any particular market. Demand is said to be either elastic or inelastic. Elasticity describes the degree to which demand will increase if prices are decreased. Of the many variables that affect demand for psychotherapy, the two important ones are availability of supply and immediacy of demand.

Just as every product and service has a unique demand associated with it, every producer has a certain quantity that will be supplied at various prices. Elasticity is also used to describe a supplier's response to an increase in price. Following this reasoning, every psychotherapist has a finite number of hours per day available to provide services. A psychotherapist's availability of hours could be described as inelastic since a therapist could not increase the number of hours available in response to an increase in price; once a maximum level is reached for an individual s/he could not expand and provide more hours. The psychotherapy industry, on the other hand, is more elastic since it represents the aggregate number of hours available for service delivery. The task for the psychotherapist who wants to become or remain competitive is to assess demand and supply of the potential market and the forces that influence them. The technique to accomplish this task is a market analysis.

When the business community talks about a market analysis they are referring to data which can answer questions concerning what goods will be produced, who will produce them, where they will be produced, and in what forms. In addition, they want to know how to best reach the consumers and what prices will be most acceptable. In short, the market analysis is concerned with first establishing whether or not there is a demand for the goods or services to be offered. In this case, demand is a technical term defined as a want which is backed by purchasing power. There must be a desire and a willingness to buy (Barkley, 1977). A market analysis would find there is no demand for air conditioners in Barrow, Alaska, because it doesn't get warm enough even in the summer for anyone to use air conditioners. An air conditioner salesperson in that area would soon go out of business. Yet, if s/he were to locate in Brownsville, Texas s/he'd stand a better chance of staying in business.

Secondly, a firm must know what the needs of the market are. Suppose the market analysis in Brownsville indicated that the residents did not like being hot in the summer it would be a prime opportunity for an air conditioning salesperson to satisfy a consumer need to be cool during the summer. On the other hand consumers might actually like experiencing the summer's heat and perhaps consider it unnatural to be cool during the warm months. In that case there is a need perceived by the seller, but not the buyer. Marketing air conditioners is still possible but the tasks involved are somewhat different.

Thirdly, the firm must know how the consumers' needs and wants are currently being satisified. Or to put it more directly, what the competition is. The market analysis in Brownsville which indicates that people cool off with ceiling fans presents a different marketing challenge than the one which shows that residents like hot weather. An air conditioning salesperson could compete with the salesperson of ceiling fans by finding out which residents were not entirely satisfied with the results of ceiling fans and sell those residents air conditioners. When selling to those with a bias against cooling the salesperson would have to identify reasons why consumers like being warm and find ways to change them.

By finding out who the consumers are, what their needs and wants are, and how these consumers are presently having their needs and wants met, a firm gets a general picture of the interaction between buyers and sellers in the industry. The firm can, then, develop a strategy for linking its goods or services with those consumers who can make best use of them.

The market analysis is a way of thinking about solving a firm's marketing problems. The point of departure is the business plan, since we must know what the mission of the firm is along with its objectives. The market analysis is a prerequisite for preparing a marketing plan, which you now recognize as an important tool for overall management of your practice.

Conducting a market analysis or what we could call an audit requires you to objectively consider a variety of pieces of information and assemble them so you can evaluate the potential of doing what you'd like to in the way of service delivery. On the basis of your audit you should have a better understanding of whether it is feasible to continue your present activities or get into other forms of service. The marketing audit is composed of several elements which are interrelated. These include analyzing and specifying the market, the competition, your organization, external opportunities and threats, and marketing strategy.

A marketing audit should be conducted regularly, perhaps once a year. We might say that the job of the market analysis is to assess the three C's: consumers, competition, and capability. Elements contained in an audit procedure are summarized in Table 1.

Table 1
SUMMARY OF PSYCHOTHERAPY PRACTICE MARKETING AUDIT

I. The Market
    A. Geographic location
        1. What is it?
        2. How big is it?
        3. How is it divided?

    B. Segmentation
        1. What are the bases for segmenting?
        2. How were they divided?
            a. ease of identification
            b. hold potential for serving
            c. adequate demand
            d. economic accessibility
            e. reactivity to marketing efforts
        3. What are the demographic and psychographic characteristics?
        4. From which sources was information obtained?
            a. own research
            b. university
            c. mental health authority

(Table 1 *continued*)

    d. health planning board
    e. utility company
    f. government office
    g. chamber of commerce
    h. *Sales and Marketing Management*
    i. other

  5. What factors limit your potential market?

C. Demand
  1. What demand states exist?
  2. What strategies are required?

II. The Competition
  A. How many competitors are there now?

  B. In what segments are they competing?

  C. What specific services are offered by your competitors?

  D. What advantages do you have over your competitors?

  E. What advantages do competitors have over you?

  F. What new sources of competition do you anticipate?

III. Opportunities & Threats
  A. What are the environmental elements?
    1. Technological innovations
    2. Governmental regulations
    3. Economy
    4. Culture
    5. Population demographics
    6. Levels of each demand state
    7. Your image

  B. How would you describe the organizational elements within your practice?
    1. Structure
    2. Systems
    3. Tasks
    4. Personnel
    5. Culture

IV. Marketing Strategy
  A. How could your marketing strategy be described?

  B. Would an alternative strategy be better suited to your practice objectives?

The Market

Geographic Area. The first step in conducting the market analysis is to establish the geographic area to be covered. Psychotherapists are limited in the area they can serve. Therapists can only provide their services in person and therefore can realistically count on servicing a territory as wide as s/he or her/his clients are willing to travel. When a therapist's reputation becomes strong clients might come from almost anywhere to receive her/his **special** treatment. Sigmund Freud enjoyed a far reaching reputation and had numerous people traveling great distances to get his services. This was also true for Milton H. Erickson, M.D., the well known hypnotherapist based in Phoenix who died in 1980.

For most of us, however, clients in proximity to the location of our practice make up our market. It should be remembered that some firms use the results of market analyses to decide on where to locate. This is not typical in the professions, although some actually do relocate based on market availability. For example, some physicians relocate to areas of high health need. Some may do so willingly out of humanitarian wishes; some require the assistance of outside agents, such as the Public Health Service with whom they have contracted to give their services in exchange for underwriting a portion of their medical education costs. Some move because they desire a change in their lifestyle. This was the case for Edward J. Carroll, M.D., who decided he was spread too thinly between teaching, serving as a training analyst, directing a treatment center for children, serving on state medical boards, and private practice so he carefully planned his move from Pennsylvania to Florida. Alan Schlaks, Ph.D., on the other hand, is one of a select group of psychotherapists who was motivated to move based on an assessment of private practice considerations. He relocated from the west coast to the east coast because he carefully assessed what he thought to be better market opportunities in the new location.

Segmentation Bases. After the geographic area has been established, either intentionally or by default, the next task is one of identifying **who** the potential consumers are, or with a little help, could be. This is not so easy for psychotherapists because we tend to believe that people in need of our services must want to receive them. If they need treatment but don't voluntarily seek it they get our sympathy and perhaps our wish that one day they will see the light. We reason further that if such people came to treatment they would not improve much because they lack sufficient motivation. The authors maintain that such a position about clients perpetuates a production-orientation that is ultimately self-defeating for therapists and fails to provide the best kind of services to our communities and our society. Identifying who the potential consumers of mental health services are is exactly what is done by public mental health authorities. The authors spent several years working in community mental agencies and were involved in conducting needs assessments, which were a major component of the agency's long-range operation plans. Like many of the tools nonprofit agency management uses, needs assessments were borrowed from our neighbors in the corporate world. If this technique is acceptable for public mental health programs there is little reason not to use it in private service delivery.

There is an almost unlimited number of ways to segment a market into meaningful clusters. These include segmenting by geography, diagnostic categories, common problems, age, gender, income groups, hobbies, patterns of consumption, price sensitivities, benefits sought, and combination of categories. In order to determine what the market population's characteristics are in ways that can be useful for developing a market strategy, it's helpful to classify them as either demographic or psychographic.

In all likelihood you are already familiar with the concept of demographics. Qualities such as age, gender, ethnicity, educational level, and income are parameters that describe a population demographically. These qualities are useful for psychotherapists to the extent they are associated with or are indicative of seeking psychotherapy services on the part of the target market. For example, people with higher levels of education are likely to seek out and respond well to insight-oriented therapy. By contrast, those with less education often respond better to short-term action oriented therapies (e.g., cognitive behavior therapy; strategic therapy). Similarly, we know that a certain income level is necessary to afford psychotherapy from a private practitioner. Yet, in some states third party payers are able to reimburse for treatment by a non-medical provider, making private services more readily available. This brings us around to a truism of market analysis: the results are only as good as the data that are entered. Computer scientists have an acronym GIGO: garbage in, garbage out which they use for describing programming. It applies to market analysis as well. The marketer of psychotherapy services must use information that is specifically relevant to her/his target market and specific situation.

The next step in the market analysis is to identify a particular group of potential consumers within the market for service delivery. We've been using the term "segment" throughout our discussion. By segment we mean a particular group of potential consumers to whom the marketer of psychotherapy would like to offer a specific therapeutic service. Segmenting may be defined as dividing the entire market into smaller clusters or sub-groups of potential consumers and developing specific strategies for them. Another way to look at this concept is as an alternative to considering everyone altogether as if people were indistinguishable in their needs and wants. Segmenting is aimed at developing meaningful clusters based on some common characteristics of a selected group which can be reached with a relatively unique marketing mix.

To illustrate what we've been talking about, let's take the example of hair cutting services. Some people cut their own hair, some people go to whatever barber shop or beauty salon is available and convenient, others go out of their way to find the most glamorous and fashionable stylist possible, and still others exhibit alternate forms of consuming these services. We can distinguish between each type of consumer on the basis of some qualities they share. For example, patrons of high fashion stylists may all have certain levels of income, live in particular neighborhoods, shop in certain kinds of department stores, regularly use one credit card, have certain hobbies and read similar magazines. These are attributes that set them apart from consumers of the other hair styling services. Knowing this information can allow us to prepare a strategy for developing or modifying our services if we want to reach them. We will also be in a better position to communicate with them if we know they share certain habitual buying and lifestyle patterns. If these people shop in one department store we might opt to locate next door. If we know they prefer one kind of credit card over all others we would make that payment method available. In essence, we would customize our services to the wants, desires, and habits of the market segment we want as consumers.

There is a wealth of literature on market segmenting and segmentation research. There is also little doubt that segmenting and then targeting is a worthwhile strategy for running a business concern. What is essential for you to know is not that psychotherpaists should go out and conduct expensive market research, but rather that therapists **think** in terms of defining who is in the market, how they might be characterized, and making an intentional effort to respond to the needs of the segment(s) you chose. Bell (1972) points out five elements of segments which can be used as a guide for decision making. They are ease of identification, holding potential as a market, demonstrating sufficient demand, economic accessibility, and distinct reactivity to marketing efforts.

Identifying a potential segment may be as simple as stating a preference for one type of client over another. This is often what therapists do. They might say, for example, the clients they want are children, or women, or victims of domestic violence. A segment might be identified by interest, by training, or even by catching the therapist's eye in the media. The last point is illustrated by an experience a colleague had. Shortly after a close friend had the unfortuante experience, this therapist read an article in a magazine on the impact death of an infant had on the parents and other family members. Subsequently, her sensitivity to the problem was heightened and she discovered there was a support group nearby, as she lived in a fairly large city. As her interest grew she began offering therapy to these families and this became a significant part of her practice. One of the nice things about being a psychotherapist is that we provide services that are useful to people who are in distress. We can change course in response to what's taking place in our communities. To identify potential segments we need simply keep our eyes and ears open and allow ourselves to be creative.

You could conduct your own market research to obtain information on your market's global characteristics, but it is hardly worth the effort and expense for this information. These data are available from secondary sources such as NIMH reports, epidemiological studies, and social area analyses. These are in the public domain and you are entitled to have access to them under the Freedom of Information Act. You might be required to purchase final reports or pay a page fee for copying, but this is still far less costly than conducting your own field research. A good starting point for getting demographic information on your target market is a mental health center or local mental health authority, such as a mental health board. These agencies go after the same kind of information that you want. They have a different use for them, however, since they are mandated to serve consumers of public mental health services. As you know, these consumers tend to be poorer, more severely disordered, and less likely candidates for psychotherapy. Some mental health centers conduct their own research while others obtain the data they need from local or regional planning boards. You can do the same thing. There are often regional health planning councils who are charged with overseeing and coordinating a wide range of services. Usually they are only too glad to give out the information they went to a lot of trouble to collect and which often sits idly on a shelf collecting dust. City and county governments also have hordes of information you can easily obtain. Some even have special offices or sections concerned with demographic and census data. After all, government offices are trying to do the same thing you are. They are gathering data which can be used for describing current conditions and used to make predictions about what may happen in the future so they can plan for change and develop the most appropriate services. If you find the right office and make a visit there you'll be amazed at the sophisticated forecasting systems that are in use. Projections are made about population shifts and economic conditions for particular geographic areas. They can be plotted on maps which give a visual representation of the region. With a little tenacity you can learn to negotiate governmental bureaucracies. You'll glean information which you can use in managing your practice. You'll also get fascinating information which can help make you become more interesting at parties.

Aside from governmental sources, demographic information can be obtained from chambers of commerce. They frequently get information from the same governmental agencies described above and can save you a lot of leg work. Information they have is geared to the business community, but part of their job is to convince businesses to consider their communities as places for potential relocation so they are less comprehensive than other sources might be. The advantage of using information from the chamber of commerce is that it is organized in ways that make them immediately comprehensible.

Additional sources of demographic data are local colleges and universities. Faculty and students in departments of sociology, geography, psychology, health education, epidemiology, and community medicine often undertake social area analysis study projects for classes and research. They might make these available to you for your work. If you are lucky and time it right, professors might be willing to have their students do a custom project for you addressing the specific questions you have. An often overlooked resource is public utility companies (Rubright & MacDonald, 1981). They perform studies of population shifts and demographic characteristics to assist in preparing proposals for rate hikes and planning to meet service demands for the future.

In 1985 the American Medical Association initiated a service for their members to aid in practice development. This service, called the Market Area Profile (MAP), contains information on demographics and health resources. Details on registering for MAP service are available from the AMA, 535 Dearborn, Chicago, IL 60610, (312) 645-4719.

There are many sources of demographic information that can be readily obtained. It is important to get as much relevant data as possible but the information may not seem relevant while it is being gathered. The best advice here is get much more than you need and ignore what you don't use. That is preferable to badly wanting a piece of information that you could have had and not being able to obtain it easily afterwards.

It is essential not to lose sight of the fact that what you are after is information that not merely describes your market, but information that describes the market in relation to the service you have to offer. If you know that there is a dominant age-race-sex group in your market this information is just descriptive of who is there. You also have to know something about their propensity to need psychotherapy as well as their willingness to seek it out. You might be able to examine your demographic data in terms of prevalence of mental and emotional disorders.

In 1978, the President's Commission on Mental Health reported that over 15% of the adult population in the United States suffers from some form of emotional disorder. That figure came as no great surprise as it was consistent with prevalence studies conducted over the past two decades. These results concerned the entire country. If you begin with that figure and think it is representative of your market you may be right. In the absence of any other information that is as good a starting point as any. Unfortunately, you may be wrong. That information may be too general for your particular market. Assume you live in a town where there is a state psychiatric hospital nearby that discharges a great number of patients directly into the community because the local mental health center runs a half-way house established under a federal grant. You may find that the prevalence of mental disorder in your community is very different from the national picture. You may also find a disproportionate number of residents who have emotional disorders, but do not require the services of psychotherapists. Instead, these consumers use the services of psychiatrists or other physicians for medication maintenance. If you are a non-medical therapist you will have to identify another group to target your services to.

Even if you are accurate in defining who might be suitable for treatment you must remember that as few as 15% of those in need ever present themselves for treatment by a mental health service provider (Regier, Goldberg, & Taub, 1978). The rest either get supportive help from clergy, social service agencies, and the like, or not at all. The most recent data on utilization of mental health service providers comes from the NIMH Epidemiological Catchment Area (ECA) program. The ECA survey was conducted in New Haven, CT, Baltimre, MD, and St. Louis, MO. One component of the project examined utilization patterns (Shapiro, et al., 1984). These results indicated that over the six-month period of study between 6% and 7% of the adults in the ECA made outpatient visits for mental health reasons. Between 2% and 4% of all visits were made to mental health specialists. The rest went to medical practitioners. As expected, a greater proportion of people with past and recent diagnosable disorders used mental health services than did those with no disorders. Sadly, a substantial number of people in emotional distress appeared to receive no appropriate treatment whatsoever.

An alternative to considering the segment of the population that actually have mental or emotional disorders and may thus require your services is to consider those who are **at risk** for developing problems at some time in the near future. You can use your imagination to identify the kinds of problems which characterize people in your market that put them at risk and then gather data to check out your hunch. In one study we came across, the investigators concluded that just under 27% of a midwestern state's entire population were at risk for emotional distress (White & Beeson, 1982). It's not clear, however, just how many of these individuals would actually seek a therapist's services but this is a useful figure to consider, especially since many practitioners provide services to people experiencing only mild adjustment related problems.

One of the best sources of information on market characteristics is the periodical, *Sales and Marketing Management.* It annually publishes information by town, city, county, and state with breakdowns by age, gender, race, income levels, and a wealth of other variables connected with buying power. This publication is generally available in public and college libraries and can provide you with economic information which can be combined with the pieces of data you've gotten from other sources.

What we've been talking about thus far concerns general characteristics of the greater environment from which you draw your clientele. The actual arrangement of characteristics in the client population you actually serve may be entirely different. The only sure way to find out about your clients is directly from them. Presumably you have some records in your files concerning your own clients. It is a simple matter to assemble them and map out the age, race, occupation, referral issue, and so on of your practice to develop a user profile. One enterprising family physician we met examined only the zip codes of her patients and on that basis was able to convince a couple of other physicians to open a satellite office that was more convenient for a large contingent of patients.

The other way of classifying characteristics of a market's population is what has been termed **psychographics,** which is concerned with attitudes, opinions, interests, and lifestyle dimensions of behavior. Psychographics was conceived by Emanuel Demby in the 1960s (Demby, 1974). When it comes to utilization of health care services, patterns of consumption and choice are determined to a greater extent by psychographic factors than by demographics, according to Wortzel (1976). This doesn't mean demographics should be ignored or downplayed in importance. On the contrary, when conducting your market analysis all information should be gathered and assembled. First you must know who is in the market before you can ascertain what attitudes and lifestyles are present, and then ascertain what their relation is to seeking a therapist's services.

Winston (1983/84) has divided psychographic/lifestyle profiling into four categories. First, is **psychological attributes** which provides information on what types of personality characteristics exist in the population or certain segments of it within the target market. Secondly, **lifestyle variables** have to do with any characteristics which people's activities can be classified into. For example, how people spend their leisure time and extra income are essential parts of lifestyle. Do they spend their time cooking gourmet food? or do they jog? or go to museums? or hang out in cutting-and-shooting bars? Third, is the **purchasing variables,** which have to do with aspects like brand loyalty. Do they drink only Pepsi or do they buy the bargain colas instead? Or, do they drink whatever cola happens to be on sale but insist on Pepsi at restaurants or when entertaining? For therapists this might mean knowing if the segment of the population that uses therapy goes on a regular basis or goes when in crisis, then drops out. Finally, there is what might be called **good/service perceptions.** These are the attitudes about characteristics of what is consumed. Perhaps a segment of the market perceives therapy as increasing their social status or, conversely, views visits to therapists as a sign of personal weakness or defectiveness.

Constructing psychographic profiles is no simple matter for the psychotherapist for two basic reasons. One, therapists have not been trained to think in terms of characterizing clients as carefully as needed, and even if they had it wouldn't matter because; two, research on psychographic profiles of clients and potential clients is virtually nonexistent. Researchers have paid a good deal of attention to characterizing people who receive psychotherapy along various parameters. There are also many studies on therapist-client interactions which facilitate treatment outcome. Although we have studies of attitudes of mentally ill people and attitudes toward mental health programming, we have no research on characteristics of people which relate to seeking therapy for personal problem-solving in non-client groups. In short, there has been a nearly complete ignoring on the part of the research community of investigations which could yield sufficient data to build psychographic profiles of significant cohorts of potential consumers of psychotherapy. Until such data become available, therapists must rely on anecdotal information and extrapolate from existing empirical data. It is also possible to conduct your own simple psychographic studies. For example, you could construct a questionnaire that you might use as part of your intake procedure or as a follow up of clients who were treated. You might include items on leisure activities (e.g., similar to those contained in the Leisure Activities Blank), fashion consciousness, church attendance, favorite stores, and so on. You could also include items focusing on specific attributes of your practice. This is a commonly used way that hospitals and other health care facilities conduct market research (Reese, Stanton, & Daley, 1982).

Demand. Psychographic profiling is a kind of applied social psychology. It's aimed at using behavioral science principles to identify certain human qualities and empirically relate them to other behaviors. The behavior we are most interested in is the propensity to seek psychotherapy. In business parlence we call such propensity **demand.** Kotler (1980) identifies eight types of demand states which characterize industrial products. Only a few are relevant to psychotherapy so we'll limit our discussion to them.

A major problem faced by therapists is **negative demand.** This demand state exists when a segment of the market actively dislikes the product or service, and may deliberately go out of their way to avoid it. Negative demand is accompanied by strong negative beliefs which may involve incorrect information as well. The marketing task in this situation is to reverse this demand state by a **conversional marketing** strategy. This approach might consist of first discovering the reasons why particular market segments hold the opinions they do and then develop a plan to convert them into opinions tha might lead to seeking therapy when there is a need. For example, a certain segment of the population might think that therapy is only for emotionally disturbed people and even if they themselves have a personal problem it doesn't mean that they are emotionally disturbed. So, they refuse to seek therapy because that would mean they are crazy and since they are convinced they are not, they don't go to a therapist and instead attempt to solve the problem the best way they know how. The conversional strategy which might be directed to this group is aimed at getting the point across that therapy is a legitimate way to solve problems and might even be beneficial in learning how to solve a variety of problems which might improve enjoyment of one's job, marriage, recreational pursuits, and so on. It might also include the argument that therapy is frequently used by successful people who are not emotionally disturbed to aid them in becoming even more successful. The goal of this kind of strategy is to overcome the biases by rational argument and correcting the erroneous view based on misinformation. To a significant degree, the negative demand state characterizes psychotherapy for many segments of our entire population.

A somewhat different condition is that of **latent demand,** wherein a perceived need exists, but there is currently no service available to meet that need. It may also indicate that whatever goods or services exist to meet the expressed needs are inadequate. Perhaps they are of inferior quality or perhaps they are of insufficient quantity. For instance, there may be a need for effective parenting skills by a group of inexperienced mothers, or a group who wishes to stop smoking cigarettes. These are demands which can be met by psychotherapists. The marketing task for a therapist facing a latent demand state is **developmental marketing** in which efforts are directed at determining what the unmet needs are and developing an appropriate service to satisfy them. Take the example of K. C., a therapist who wanted to expand his practice to serve smokers wishing to quit. After determining there was a large enough number of smokers who wanted to quit and could afford to obtain treatment, he examined the competition. He found there were half a dozen different types of smoking cessation programs currently available in the community, each with a different focus and different cost. However, none were currently using hypnosis in their service, so he decided to offer smoking cessation treatment with hypnosis. The target segment consisted of those smokers who'd tried other methods but had not been successful Since no other method included hypnosis, K. C. targeted a group of potential consumers who remained motivated to seek additional treatment.

Finally, there is the state of **irregular demand.** These states are characterized by fluctuations. Most restaurants have fluctuating demand depending on the time of day. Florists, retail jewelers, and furriers experience changes in sales reflecting changes in season and holidays. Similarly, the psychotherapist finds changes in patterns of service use which vary with seasons and holidays. In summer months when many people take vacations, clients often cancel or stop treatment briefly for a trip or visit from friends and relatives. Sometimes clients work toward termination prior to holidays also. In addition, some holidays, like Christmas, bring on an increase of referrals for some therapists. The marketing task for this irregular demand state is what Kotler (1980) terms **synchromarketing.** This simply means synchronizing supply and demand so they are better integrated to avoid too much demand which cannot be met or an overabundant supply. For psychotherapists, it could mean anticipating fluctuations and juggling schedules and caseloads. Perhaps the day will arrive when therapists have special prices for off-peak times the way that restaurants offer "early bird specials."

Unfortunately, just because you've identified a segment you might be interested in, focusing attention on it does not mean that you can or should direct considerable efforts to capturing it. First you must be sure there is enough demand to justify spending the requisite resources (time, energy, money). This decision begins with a simple head count (we'll worry about the competition later). Are there enough potential clients in the identified segment of this market for a therapist to treat? — is the question which addresses this element. If you are satisfied that there are enough potential clients, you must identify the demand state present within the segment. It is possible that several demand states exist within the same segment. Consider the situation of a therapist who decides on victims of sexual assault as an appropriate segment. Some rape victims will avoid therapy since they have reached a denial phase in the predictable progression of adjustment responses. For them therapy may be characterized as having a negative demand. Therapy is actively avoided because there is the perception of psychological well-being. Another segment of rape victims is in the symptom-formation stage (Forman, 1980) and may view therapy as desirable. For them, latent demand exists. They want treatment for a particular kind of problem which may or may not be available to them.

When we are reasonably sure we've identified the demand states that are present in our chosen segment we simultaneously have determined, in a global sort of way, what the marketing task is. Yet, before we go any further in pursuing this segment we have to establish the segment's economic viability. Having identified single women over the age of 35 who are employed as middle managers, as a segment for marketing stress management programs, virtually guarantees the ability to pay for services. The therapist who wants to provide therapy to rape victims is less certain of this segment's ability to pay private rates. S/he must then specify the segment more clearly, be prepared to alter service features, or adjust fees. All these modifications are legitimate ways to manage segmenting. In fact, it's doubtful that any therapist would deny services to a rape victim or any one else who needs services simply because of inability to pay. By careful consideration of the segments we target, we can be in a better position to assure that your practice has a comfortable balance of clients.

The Competition

Psychotherapy services are available in most communities from public mental health agencies, non-profit agencies, and private practitioners. It's relatively easy to obtain information on who's providing services and what kind of services are being offered in publically-supported agencies since all this information is in the public domain. You can get it directly from these agencies or from local or state mental health authorities. It's slightly more difficult to get information from non-governmental agencies. Some of these are supported by United Way or other charitable organizations and routinely make this kind of information available to members of the public to show what a good job they are doing with donations. Family service agencies, for example, have such sponsorship and prepare annual reports which are often available upon request. Getting information from church-sponsored counseling programs may take nothing short of a dispensation from a higher authority. Among private practitioners the number and types of clients treated are generally regarded as quite confidential, but can often be obtained through ingenuity and tenacity. Participating in professional associations is a major way therapists get to know one another and we are likely to share information with colleagues well known to us.

Opportunity vs. Risk

It is also necessary to consider those factors that will impinge upon your potential to enter a new market or expand services to an existing one that you're currently serving. In conducting your opportunity analysis there are two domains that are included for assessing strengths and weaknesses. These are the environment and the internal organization.

The environment includes the community, the greater society, and the profession among elements that influence your practice. The specific areas to address are as follows:

1. Technology Innovation. Whatever the current developments in psychotherapy and counseling research and methods that are becoming prominent should be considered. If you're among the practitioners who've developed some new techniques, have contributed to theory, or cultivated a specialization you might chalk up a plus for opportunity. On the other hand you may be limiting yourself by overspecializing. The methods you use may be falling into disfavor with respect to increasing emphasis on biochemical interventions and neuropsychological advances.

2. Goverment. Here you consider the status of governmental and regulatory agencies at local, state, and national levels. You must consider the current legislation affecting the profession in general as well as that pertaining to your specific discipline. So you might want to look at current laws on licensure and certification. For example, regulation of marriage and family therapists is increasing throughout the U.S. These laws will regulate entry into the profession, the supply, and could influence one's ability to receive third party payments. Tax incentives in the form of personal income tax deductions for therapy is another area for study.

3. Economics. The national economic trends act upon all of us in many spheres of our lives. The current state of the economy is about the only surefire index of what the economy is doing, since it is already doing so. Your ability to forecast accurately about the economy is no worse than economists who are engaged in folie a deauxs with one another but have numbers attached to their delusions to lull the rest of us into thinking it's social science they practice. There's little agreement among economists anyway. As George Bernard Shaw once said, "If all economists were laid end to end, they would not reach a conclusion." Economic forecasting fiascos notwithstanding, the current state of the economy surely influences whether or not therapy is affordable, how the cash flow of your market runs, the amount of credit buying your market engages in, and whether or not your clients are going to pay you.

4. Culture. The locale of your practice as well as social trends are going to impact on your practice's viability. In times of stress, referrals to therapists are likely to increase but only among persons for whom therapy is acceptable. There was a time when going to psychoanalysts was popular, particulaly among financially successful urbanites. You should consider the prevailing attitudes and values in your community and tie them to cultural concerns and practices among varying ethnic groups.

5. Demographics. Baby boomers have grown up and the population at large is getting older. While this may hold for the entire country your market may have a dramatically different arrangement. The factors creating the distinct pattern are of marginal interest for your market audit, since this relates data to what currently exists. If you are aware of any factors that will influence the local population characteristics, put them in your market plan.

6. Competition. You've already assessed the competition in terms of who they are and what segments they are serving. At this point you must evaluate your image, how clear it is, if you are perceived as having a service that makes you stand out among the others, and what kinds of services the others provide that could adversely affect your position.

7. Demand. Now you designate the particular demand states of the market segments you hope to reach along with those of the segments you already serve. You can characterize the demand as being for new services, replacement/alternative services, or as latent, seasonal, and so forth.

The second set of elements to include in your opportunity vs. risk analysis is concerned with the internal environment of your practice. Here, we're concerned with the organizational components and how they interact. A conceptual framework developed by the Management Analysis Center, a consulting firm, offers a useful tool for understanding the workings of any organization (Aaker, 1984). This model includes the following five components.

1. Structure. Lines of authority and communication as well as definitions of roles and functions are included in an organization's structure. In addition, assignments of tasks and their coordination are also parts of the structure. In the psychotherapy practice there are usually few personnel other than the therapist. Nonetheless, all the managerial responsibilties found in large firms are necessary for therapists, even those in solo practice.

2. Systems. Operating procedures, budgeting, record keeping, scheduling, insurance claim filing, and planning are different types of systems. You may want to consider as strengths those systems that are standardized and routine so they work efficiently. Weaknesses may be any that have not been thought out and require re-thinking so your operation runs smoothly.

3. Tasks. The major task of the psychotherapist is to treat clients. Yet, if the other tasks connected with running an efficient organization are not adequately dealt with you will not be able to stay in business. The accounting, marketing, record keeping functions are every bit as important to the longevity of your practice as are your therapy skills. This is why we hear about therapists with adequate therapy skills reducing their practices and seeking jobs. Each therapist is unique and has areas of professional strengths as well as certain deficits. Before s/he can hope to fill an existing need within a market segment s/he must have the capabilities to do so. Suppose the therapist who identifies a segment with a need for non-medical approaches to pain management has no experience with medical populations and no familiarity with pain management methods. At this point in time it would be foolhearty, not to mention unethical, to begin targeting that segment. S/he would first be obliged to review her/his qualifications to do such work and then take steps to upgrade her/his skills. It's difficult to be objective about one's capabilities, particularly when we are as ego-invested in our skills as therapists. It is essential that we view our technical expertise as machinery and inventory for production so we can accurately specify both strengths and weaknesses.

4. People. In such a people-oriented profession as psychotherapy, social skills are considered relatively high. At least that's what we'd like to believe because we are concerned with the quality of life for others. Yet, therapists can be just as inept as anyone else in terms of managing the human resources in our practices. We are interested in our own experiences and skills, but we do not typically have formal policies about personnel matters for our practices. Nor do we think about staffing patterns, abilities, or expectations concerning bringing on associates. Although most practitioners do not have full-time secretarial staff, those that do employ them typically do not devote the same attention to their professional development as is devoted to treatment staff.

5. Culture. Culture refers to the psychological climate of your practice. Every organization, no matter how small, has its very own culture much the same as individuals have unique personalities. Your attitudes about clients, values, relationships with staff, ways of resolving conflicts, and general managerial style form the culture of your practice.

Once you've delineated how your organization has weaknesses and strengths in each of the above components, the next step is to consider the interactions. For example, you might pose the questions suggested by Aaker (1984). "Do the systems fit the structure?" "Do the people fit the culture?" "Do the people fit the structure?" "Does the structure fit the culture?" "Do the people fit the tasks?"

Marketing Strategy

Finally, Bell (1972) advises that we have differing marketing strategies suitable for each segment. In other words, we ought to ascertain whether the segment we've chosen is responsive to the promotional tools and marketing mix we've selected. Suppose we've chosen well-educated, professional, upper income consumers for our target segment. A marketing strategy directed to the exclusivity motive is more suitable than a strategy based on low cost. Features such as premium price, luxurious office furnishings, and other trappings of success and high achievement are likely to appeal to this segment much more than the segment that is primarily seeking moderate costs associated with treatment. On the other hand, if you're targeting to a cost-conscious segment, a more appropriate strategy could be locating your practice in or near a discount department store and furnished with utilitarian styled furniture. This approach was effective for dental practitioners. In a recently published study, consumer use of "retail dentists" was motivated largely by the lower fees charged by this group (Trauner, Luft, & Robinson, 1982).

CHAPTER SUMMARY

Psychotherapy services, like manufactured goods, have levels of demand associated with them at varying prices within different markets. The supply of services, defined as number of hours of therapist availability, varies with demand. An individual's supply is finite but the supply within the industry is comparatively unlimited.

Conducting a market analysis or audit involves defining the forces that affect supply and demand within a selected market. The results are a useful management tool for developing or refocusing marketing strategies. The audit process involves (1) specifying the market's geographic location, meaningful segments, and their associated demand states, (2) identifying sources of competition, (3) analyzing opportunities and threats both in the external environment and within the practice, (4) determining ways in which strategies have been implemented to address the market characteristics as they exist.

The geographic area of each therapist's market is typically limited to the distance clients are willing to travel. In urban areas with higher concentrations of both clients and therapists the distance may be smaller than in more rural locations. Forces of supply and demand are the significant determinants here.

Within each market, segmenting can be useful for remaining competitive since you can determine the best way to position your practice and differentiate your services from those of your competitors. Bases for creating segments can be classified as either demographic or psychographic. Demographic characteristics refer to broad physical and social features such as age, gender, educational level, occupation, and diagnostic categories. Psychographic characteristics are defined as values and lifestyle dimensions of behavior, which are better than either demographic or personality variables for predicting consumer behavior, particularly in health care. Included among psychographics are hobbies, type of benefits sought from the service, and social values.

Each segment has a demand state which characterizes its orientation to any good or service. Common demand states which present challenges to marketers of psychotherapy are negative demand, latent demand, and irregular demand. Negative demand is when there are attitudes and opinions which inhibit utilization of services. It is addressed by a strategy aimed at converting the segment's beliefs. Latent demand is when a need for psychotherapy exists but cannot be met adequately. A marketing strategy termed developmental is used in which ways to tap the unmet needs are formulated. Irregular demand states are those that fluctuate with time of day, season, or some other factor. Synchromarketing is used to match the pattern of the demand state by anticipating when these fluctuations will occur and responding to them.

Analyzing the competition requires you to define all sources of service delivery available within your market. These will include both public and private providers who offer services to the segments you serve as well as other segments. It is recommended that you also consider the marketing strategies your competitors are using plus any plans they have for expanding into other segments.

Opportunities and risks come from a host of other sources. You can consider them as lying either in the enviornment or within the organization and evaluate the strengths and weaknesses you have for dealing with them. Among the environmental elements are advances or innovations in the field of psychotherapy, governmental regulations, the general economy, the social and cultural milieu, population demographics, your image vis-a-vis the competition, and levels of each demand state for therapy within your market. Within your practice itself it is useful to consider the organizational components and the process by which they interact. These components are structure, which refers to lines of authority and communication along with role functions; systems, which are concerned with record keeping, budgeting, and basic operating procedures; tasks, which extend beyond those connected with client care to include all the business related activities; personnel, which includes the number and type of staff and, in addition, managing and enhancing them; culture, which is concerned with norms, values and general managerial style.

The final task within the market analysis is to examine the marketing strategy. There should be a goodness of fit between overall approach to reaching a selected segment and the characteristics of the segment itself. In essence, we check to determine the segment's responsiveness to our marketing efforts.

CASE EXAMPLE

When Charlie Plyler finished his psychiatric residency in 1968 he decided to set up practice in San Antonio, TX. He understood that the population was growing and there was a need for all medical specialties. Charlie had been in general medical practice after finishing his degree, so he had the experience of getting a practice started. He describes his method as the "standard medical approach" to practice, which involves knowing three or four physicians to get referrals from, joining the medical society; going out and talking to people. He knew that his clients were other physicians from whom he'd get referrals so he was able to identify that beyond being sociable and competent, the most important need was availability. The first professional act he performed after moving to San Antonio was to deliver a baby. "That's a crazy way to start a psychiatric practice," Charlie says. Nonetheless, he had a full practice in about three weeks.

There was more ignorance about emotional disorders in the 1960s compared to now, so the demand state that existed for Charlie Plyler's services was no different than anyone else's would have been then. Even among physicians there was something of a negative demand state. When Charlie had patients hospitalized on the psychiatric floor of one of the hospitals where he had privileges, he'd make rounds in the mornings. Then, he visited with other physicians and surgeons and talked with them about **their** work. He was genuinely interested in what was going on in other areas of medical practice and thus had the opportunity to keep up with the field. He also had the opportunity to educate the other physicians about what psychiatrists were doing and what he personally was doing with the patients he treated.

In Charlie's view, psychiatry is a sub-specialty of internal medicine, yet is a rather unique one. He maintains that developing a psychiatric practice is more difficult than establishing a practice in other specializations, like ENT. Suppose a physician is experiencing some personal depression. That's not the kind of thing that will be discussed openly with a colleague on the golf course. Even if the subject came up, neither wants to meet in the psychiatrist's waiting room. Or worse still, neither wants to run into one of their own patients in the psychiatrist's waiting room. So if a physician gets psychiatric treatment for her/himself or for family members, referrals from them virtually dies until treatment is over. This phenomenon almost never happens with other specialties.

A couple of years after coming to San Antonio, Charlie got a clinical faculty appointment at the University of Texas Medical School branch. He's not able to pinpoint specifically where this benefited his practice but knows that it helped contribute to his image and credibility.

When he first started out, Charlie considered himself a generalist. The referrals pretty much dictated the direction of his practice which were, by and large, adult outpatients who required psychotherapy. So, Charlie developed and maintained his skills as a psychotherapist but, by the late 1970s, the field of psychiatry had undergone a dramatic change where it had come to be dominated by chemical treatments. Since he had a solid background in medicine and had kept up his interests in medical practice Charlie was able to revise his methods and stay current in his understanding of drug use. Because of his background as a psychotherapist and firm belief that psychotherapists have a mission "to improve the quality of life for people," to this day, just about everything he does "has some element of psychotherapy in it."

REFERENCES

Aaker, D. A. (1984), *Strategic market management.* New York: Wiley.

Barkley, P. W. (1977), *Introduction to microeconomics.* New York: Harcourt Brace Jovanovich.

Bell, M. L. (1972), *Marketing: Concepts and strategy.* Boston: Houghton-Mifflin.

Demby, E. (1974) Psychographics and from whence it came. In W. D. Wells (Ed.) *Life style and psychographics.* Chapter 1, 9-30.

Foote, N. N. (1969), Marketing segmentation as a competitive strategy. In L. Bogart (Ed.) *Current controversies in marketing research.* Chicago: Markham. 129-139.

Forman, B. D. (1980), Psychotherapy with rape victims. *Psychotherapy: Theory, Research, and Practice, 14,* 304-311.

Kotler, P. (1980), *Marketing management: Analysis, planning and control.* Englewood Cliffs, NJ: Prentice-Hall.

Reese, R. M., Stanton, W. W., & Daley, J. M. (1982), Identifying market segments within a health care delivery system: A two stage methodology. *Journal of Health Care Marketing, 2* (3), 10-23.

Regier, D. A., Goldberg, I. D. & Taub C. A. (1978), The defacto U.S. mental health services system. *Archives of General Psychiatry, 35,* 685-693.

Shapiro, S., Skinner, E. A., Kessler, L. G., VonKorff, M., German, P. S., Tischler, G. L., Leof, P. J., Benham, L., Cottler, L., & Regier, D. A. (1984), Utilization of health and mental health services. *Archives of General Psychiatry, 41,* 971-978.

Trauner, J. B., Luft, H. S., & Robinson, J. O. (1982), *Entrepreneurial trends in health care delivery: The development of retail dentistry and free standing ambulatory services.* U. S. Department of Commerce, National Technical Information Service, P.B.83-175505.

White, L. K. & Beeson, P. G. (1982), The mental health status of Nebraskans. Fifth Nebraska Annual Social Indicators Survey, Bureau of Sociological Research, University of Nebraska, Lincoln, NE.

Winston, W. J. (1983-84), Psychographic/life-style aspects for target marketing. *Health Marketing Quarterly, 1* (2/3), 19-26.

Wortzel, L. H. (1976), The behavior of the health care consumer: A selective review. In B. B. Anderson (Ed) *Advances in consumer research. Vol. III.* Association of Consumer Research.

CHAPTER 5

THE MARKETING MIX

WHEN DEVELOPING marketing plans, marketers frequently talk about place, price, product and promotion. These elements are commonly referred to as the four P's of marketing. They are considered controllable since these elements can be manipulated by the marketer in such a way as to provide the desired product, at an apropriate place at an acceptable price, using reasonable promotional activities aimed at a specific target market. The way in which these elements are assembled is called the **marketing mix,** a term coined by Harvard Business School professor Neil Borden in the late 1940s (Borden, 1964). It's essential for you to know the marketing mix so you can gain better understanding of the elements to use in developing a sophisticated marketing system for your practice.

The concept of the four P's of marketing has been used, until recently, primarily to describe the marketing mix of tangible products. Although this concept of the marketing mix can be appropriately applied to intangible services as well, we'd like to offer a slight modification.

For the purposes of discussing psychotherapy, a schema which includes "service features" and "promotion" is suggested. Service features of psychotherapy include place, price, and product, since all are actually part of delivering the service itself. Although some promotional aspects of a marketing mix are also part of the service, these activities are largely separate from service delivery. So discussing service characteristics as distinct from promotional activities allows us to focus on them more clearly.

The marketing mix elements and their characteristics are shown in Table 2. They can be useful for preparing strategies to meet marketing goals.

Table 2

MARKETING MIX ELEMENTS AND THEIR CHARACTERISTICS

Service Features

Place

location	decor & layout	access via public transportation
size	furnishings	access via thoroughfares
physical barriers	psychological barriers	parking
practice name	avenues of entry	

Price

monetary costs (fees)	opportunity costs
reception interactions	travel time
waiting time	physical comfort
psychological safety	

Product

tangibility	treatment duration	session length
therapist (personality, ability, style, appearance)	modality (individual, group; family)	orientation (e.g., RET, TA, NLP)
provider type/discipline	benefit objective	

practice style (solo, group; clinic)

peripheral services (e.g., testing, career counseling, medications, educational workshops)

Promotion

Sales Promotion

information/referral services	workshops
free/low cost first visits	brochures
promotional letters & announcements	not billing for service rendered

Personal Sales

social/recreational interactions	giving talks
treating family members of referral agents	serving on boards
client follow up activities	professional association activities

(Table 2 *continued*)

Advertising

| radio | television | newspapers | directories |

Publicity

Public Service Announcements	talk shows
news releases	own copy in media
conducting workshops	interviews with reporters

Place. When we speak of place for delivery of goods we are referring to a physical location: a store, a catalog, a vending machine. The concept of place involves the channel of distribution, or how the goods are moved from producer to consumer. Channels of distribution describe routes for the forward movement of goods, and, depending on the complexity, can have several levels ranging from zero-level in which the producer sells directly to the consumer to a three-level channel where there are three intermediaries (Kotler, 1980). These channels make goods available and accessible to target markets.

Channels of distribution can be described as being the following: zero-level, one-level, two-level, or three-level. As mentioned above, in a zero-level channel the producer sells directly to the consumer. In a one-level channel, the producer sells to the retailer who in turn sells to the consumer. In a two-level channel a consumer can get the products from a wholesaler in addition to the retailer. A three-level channel includes a jobber in addition to the wholesaler and the retailer. A jobber is a person who stocks and maintains certain shelves in a retail store, e.g., panty hose or candy or convenience stores.

Service industries also have channels of distribution, and although the industry has been characterized by a zero-level channel in which the therapist produced and sold the service directly to the consumer, most of the therapists we interviewed use at least a two-level channel and sometimes a three-level channel in delivering their services. These channels include individual and group therapy, training, professional affiliations, civic activities, and television appearances. Each of these channels is a different medium for service delivery and has a different audience or consumer group. There is some overlap here with promotion.

Place for service specifies the extent and mode of access (MacStravic, 1977). Place for psychotherapy includes the physical location with its office accoutriments. The size, decor, office layout, furnishings, and type of location are obvious characteristics of place. They communicate specific information to actual and potential clients, as well as to referral agents. Some clients will have distinct preferences for the aspects of place a therapist considers appealing, while others will have negative reactions to the same office trappings and location.

Place is also concerned with accessibility (Kotler, 1980). Accessibility relates to transportation availability as well as ease in obtaining services. That is, can a client easily get to a therapist's office? Or, are there barriers which prevent a client from seeking psychotherapy? If a client feels overwhelmed by either physical or psychological obstacles when coming for an appointment, s/he may be less motivated to return for further appointments. David Gelhof, M.D. of Chicago, finds it valuable to have an exit from his consulting room directly to the receptionist's office which leads to the corridor. In this way his patients do not have to meet one another so the potential for embarassment is minimized. This arrangement conveys a clear message from the therapist that says "I respect your right to privacy" and thereby reduces a common psychological barrier to continuing treatment.

Mone (1983) suggests that the availability of public transportation is a significant factor to be considered when deciding on office location. This would be particularly true in an urban area where there is greater reliance on this mode of transportation for mobility. Such a consideration is also more significant for certain market segments, like elderly clients.

Parking availability for clients who drive their own cars is another important consideration. Free parking is viewed as the optimal arrangement (Mone, 1983). One therapist we interviewed was in the process of moving her office. When asked why she was moving, she responded that parking was a problem in her current location; therefore, she was moving to a different location which offers more parking for clients and she is thereby modifying an essential service feature.

Ease of access via public transportation, and the convenient use of streets and highways to reach the office should be considered as general guidelines for place but it is more important to identify and respond to the specific place requirements of your target segment.

Hours of operation are another part of place. Conventional wisdom held that if clients were not willing to undergo some hardships in the course of securing psychological help they did not possess sufficient motivation to undertake the lengthy and arduous process of therapy. Even if all therapists agree in principle with the logic and veracity of such thinking, the mere forces of competition will prevail. Should you not modify your hours of availability surely some of your competitors will. If your target market is made up of people who are likely to work during daily business hours, you might consider offering evening hours for them as an appropriate adjustment in place. One therapist hired a part-time associate to offer services during the evening and on weekends, a common way of expanding hours of availability. Similarly, mothers of school age children may find it easier to keep morning appointments while children are in school. Thus, hours of operation or greatest activity may be peculiar to certain target segments.

Trauner, Luft, and Robinson (1982) report on the pioneering use of place by dentists. Beginning in 1977, dentists began locating their practices in department, discount, and drug stores. The place features they modified included extended hours of operation, free parking, pleasant decor, and no appointment required. These practices have been very successful and have spawned free standing dental offices in shopping centers.

A frequently overlooked part of place is the practice name. Most of us follow a practice naming procedure we consider discreet and professional. We use names like "Joe Dokes, Ph.D." or "Suzie Glutz, M.D., P.A." for solo practices, and "Psychotherapy Associates" for group practices. These names are adequate but do not take advantage of the marketing opportunity connected with place. For instance, Amber Goldstein, ACSW, and her colleagues wanted to provide specific services to people with phobias and called their operation a "Phobia Clinic." Granted, some potential clients would be afraid to go to such a practice for fear of being labelled. Yet, many others who make up the target segment receive a message saying "here's the place for you" simply by the title. Psychologist Carey Washington, Ph.D., has a hunch that some clients who obtained his name from the yellow pages were responding to the image of honesty and trustworthiness his name evokes.

One last point about place is an elaboration of the avenues for entry. Avenues for client referrals are a very important part of place; because without client referrals a practitioner cannot stay in business. Determining whether the target segment is self-referred, physician-referred, court-referred, and the like is an ingredient of place. In short, place includes all the activities required to arrive at and leave from the location in which therapy is provided, in addition to physical location and accomodations of the office.

Price. The word "price" has always meant just one thing to people: the monetary cost of a product or service. The definition of "cost" is the value given up for the product or service obtained. This value may have little relationsip to the cash outlay. For instance, if you wanted to buy a painting and all you had to give in exchange for the painting was a cow; the cost of the painting to you would be the cow. Therefore, price and cost are not the same. Although price to a producer includes the cost of manufacturing the product or service, it includes much more to the consumer (MacStravic, 1977). In thinking about price for psychotherapy services, in addition to the monetary payment for the service, time for travel and waiting, and personal comfort factors must be considered as well.

If a client has to travel several miles in heavy traffic over poorly maintained streets and highways and then have to hassle with parking, the price may be too high. Since, at this point, price and place overlap, careful consideration may need to be given to office location both in general and with regard to target segments.

Should a client have to wait once s/he arrived for an appointment, it may not be worth it from her/his point of view to continue treatment with you. Consequently, the client may decide to seek out another therapist for services whose associated costs are less than yours. In the past several years, the cost of waiting has gained national attention because people who have had to wait after arriving for an appointment have begun billing the professional person for the waiting time. With the help of the courts, they have received compensation too.

Manner of office staff is another component which enters into the price for the service. Careful attention to the treatment of clients by office staff is critical. No client of an attorney or real estate agent would appreciate a discourteous reception. For psychotherapy clients, demeaner of office staff is even more important because of the nature of these clients. A related factor is how the client's needs are anticipated and met. Many therapists now make efforts to discourage their clients from smoking and do not permit smoking at all in their waiting and consulting rooms. Knowing that this prohibition adds to clients' anxiety, Edmund Cava, M.D. keeps a water cooler in his waiting room. For many years Enrique Alvarez, M.D., of Goldsboro, N.C., has kept complimentary beverages such as coffee and orange juice in his waiting room.

Another element of price is opportunity costs. This is simply the consideration of other kinds of activities which might be substituted for a therapy session at the same time. Other activities may be related to meeting personal goals for which therapy was sought, such as going to another therapist or attending a couples communication seminar sponsored by a church.

Other favored activities which may be chose over therapy, and may be completely unrelated to therapy, might be watching Monday night football, playing bridge, or staying at one's job. There must be the perception that therapy is a worthwhile way to spend time or the client will eventually devote time to the activities having greater payoffs.

There are costs in terms of personal risk that therapists more than most other professionals are aware of. These are aspects of the service itself that involve personal disclosure, dependency, possible loss of dignity, or perceived intrusiveness which occur as the therapeutic relationship develops. Although we don't usually think of such characteristics of our service as a cost, they surely are as much as monetary payments.

Virtually all elements of price are controllable since there are no fixed costs in the manufacture of psychotherapy and therefore they can be modified by a therapist. Therapists can choose practice locations that maximize accessibility for their clients and can alter workstyles to maximize privacy. When there is going to be an extended waiting period, information might be provided to clients. Even therapeutic interactions can be altered to avoid intrusiveness. The most obvious modification in price is in fee structure. Increasing or reducing fees should be given careful consideration, however, since it must be kept in line with the segment selected for the practice. In addition, establishing a fee structure that is substantially lower than other practitioners operating in the same market has the potential for backfiring for two reasons. First, several insurance carriers have taken the position that discounted fees or those where a co-payment is waived are not usual and customary fees (Trauner et al., 1982). The insurers then use the reduced fee as the basis for calculating a reimbursement rate which will be lower than it was previously. Thus the lower fees could have the effect of reducing income. Second, reducing fees to a rate that is viewed by potential consumers as too low raises suspicion which may result in decreased utilization. Thomas (1978) reports that once an operator of an aviation maintenance service decided to lower his rates in the hopes of generating more business, much to his chagrin, business fell way off. When he checked with pilots who were former patrons he discovered that many believed quality was lowered to save costs. Rather than risk their lives with inferior quality these pilots decided to switch to another maintenance company instead.

Product. Psychotherapy occupies a unique position among services because the intangible results are based on a personal relationship. As a service therapy is quite different from that offered by a plumber or a dentist where there are some visible and tangible effects of the service performed. Having a leaky pipe repaired or a tooth filled are obvious to anyone who cares to make an inspection. Having a phobia removed by a therapist is possible, but difficult to demonstrate to anyone but the client. Furthermore, as we know from experience with some agoraphobics, sometimes it is even difficult to convince clients despite actual changes in their customary behavior. In some ways the services of a therapist are like those of a travel agent. One seeks the assistance of a travel agent for help in arranging a vacation. There is an implication that the vacation will be enjoyable, which is an intangible quality. Making arrangements for transportation and accommodations are important parts of the vacation but cannot be considered the service itself any more than sitting in a therapist's office is the service. Both the travel agent and the therapist use various tools and combinations of services to make good on the promise of an intangible entity which is defined as successful or unsuccessful according to the client's subjective evaluation.

Theodore Levitt (1981) argues that all products have both tangible and intangible qualities. He goes on to suggest that making the intangible features take on tangible qualities can be a useful strategy for marketing. For instance, a characteristic of automobiles is seating. Different seat types have different comfort qualities associated with them. Comfort of course is an intangible attribute and is subjective. One person finds comfort in a soft cushiony seat while another prefers a seat with firm lumbar support. Either of these seat types can be described to consumers according to materials used in their manufacture and have numbers attached to these descriptions to back up comfort claims. This is a simple way of tangibilizing the intangible. Many psychologists rely on tests for use in diagnosis and treatment planning. For most psychologists, testing represents a data-based approach to providing professional services, an outgrowth of the scientist-practitioner training model. Testing can also be thought of as a way of giving intangible client characteristics tangible qualities. Transforming personal attributes into scores on scales, that can be depicted visually to the client, gives some concrete anchors for understanding their own functioning. Suggestions made to the client based on test results have added credibility. Similarly, diplomas, certificates, and awards hanging on office walls attest to the therapist's worthiness for doing the job in the eyes of most clients.

The tangibility of psychotherapy which is often overlooked is the therapist. The therapist is the only measure of the service a potential client has. Therefore, to a large extent the therapist is the tangible service.

Alan Raphael, Ph.D., of Coral Gables, FL, who was interviewed by the authors, shared with us his three A's of success: **availability, affability,** and **appearance.** These elements coupled with Kotler's (1981) notion **accessibility** of service and the old physician's yarn which includes **ability** could be considered the five "A's" of successful psychotherapy practice.

Elements of a product or service are modified in repsonse to needs and wants of the target segment. The marketer of soft drinks for those who are both weight and taste conscious alters the product by providing a varied line of flavors or introduces artificial sweeteners without aftertaste. Recently, soft drink manufacturers identified a sizeable number of people who wanted soda without caffeine. They responded by producing a line of caffeine-free products. One producer emphasized this overlooked feature in an advertising campaign with the slogan, "Never had it, never will."

Services can be similarly modified. A few years ago commercial airlines introduced "no frills" flights for consumers wanting to travel with costs kept to a minimum. Dentists and lawyers have made similar modifications in their services. Dentists have opened practices in shopping malls with an eye on keeping costs down. By doing so they have passed the savings on to their patients who represent a market segment of people who consider reduced cost an essential part of the service features (Trauner, et al., 1982). Likewise lawyers have offered low cost legal clinics for people with certain kinds of problems (e.g., uncontested divorces) who require a fixed number of hours of service. Recently, an article in *The Wall Street Journal* (Hertzberg, 1984) reported that some banks were beginning to offer "no-frills" banking service which, of course, would be less expensive for the consumer. The "no frills" banking service requires that the customers conduct the majority of their banking business at a automated teller, although, they could have two contact visits per month in the bank. The "no frills" service is an attempt to reduce the number of costs with tellers, and, consequently, reduce the cost of servicing the account.

Promotion

As we said earlier, marketing is fundamentally a communication process between buyers and sellers. Up to now we've emphasized those parts of the interchange concerned with finding information about segments, cataloging their needs and wants, and designing suitable service features. Once these tasks are completed you are ready to send a message to consumers, letting them know you've responded to their needs in ways that are consistent with your marketing objectives. Your communication with potential consumers is termed "promotion." Its purpose is to educate, persuade, inform, or remind the target market about various aspects of your services. Perhaps you've decided to modify your hours of operation or change your therapy focus to appeal to a segment. Your goal would be to inform these potential consumers of these changes in ways that are most appropriate for them to receive this information.

Promotion is not simply getting known in the community by offering effective therapy or running some ads in the local newspaper, although we have met many therapists who believe that's all there is to it. Like most successful business practices, promotional activites should be part of a plan and the strategies used should be goal-directed. A simple model can help us in thinking about the communication process:

$$\text{WHO} \longrightarrow \text{SAYS WHAT} \longrightarrow \text{HOW} \longrightarrow \text{TO WHOM}$$
$$\uparrow \underline{\qquad} \text{WITH WHAT EFFECT} \quad < \underline{\qquad}$$

This conception is basic social psychology theory and includes all necessary elements to consider when you wish to construct and deliver a message. As the orignator of the message, you are the "who" and you determine what the message is to be, or the "what." A significant part of the message is the channel of communication which should be geared to the receivers, presumably based on careful assessment. Finally the effects of the message are noted and fed back to the originator for correction or continuation. As therapists we are all professional communicators. In our work with clients we are constantly communicating and getting feedback on the messages we send. For example, when a new client enters the office, the therapist may ask him/her to state the reasons for coming. Then the therapist listens to the explanation and, at the same time, observes the client's emotional level. This information is then integrated into the interview. Experienced therapists engage in this kind of behavior almost intuitively so we are not usually cognizant of the refined communicational skills we possess. The general public is not nearly as sophisticated as communicators. By the same token nonprofessional marketers are easily intimidated by the seeming complexity of promotional communication. But they need not be, particularly if they are therapists because therapists already are extraordinarily good a communication and must simply transfer skills from one context to another.

Marketers use the term promotional channels when referring to categories of techniques for communicating with market segments. There are four basic types of promotional channels: sales promotion, personal selling, publicity, and advertising. We realize that the terms "sales" and "selling" may offend the sensibilities of some readers as they connote seemingly unethical practices for therapists. We wish only to educate readers about some basics of marketing. We do not recommend that anyone attempt to apply all of the concepts that are discussed. Rather, we hope that you will develop a framework for thinking about your marketing efforts and employ only those which are consistent with your personal values and you are comfortable with.

As members of a highly industrialized and consumption-oriented culture each of us has been exposed to all four promotional channels. Some of our professional colleagues have already made use of them in their marketing efforts. Some examples of their creativity will be shared with you.

Sales Promotion may be defined as the use of short-term incentives to encourage or incease business volume. The incentives most often used consist of tools such as contests, premiums, demonstrations, introductory offers, and rebates. These are used regularly in promotions as anyone who watches television or reads newspapers well knows. Book clubs and publishers have used this technique for many years as a means of enrolling subscribers. Incentives have not been used very much in the psychotherapy business but they are just beginning to get some recognition among our suppliers. For instance, several psychological test scoring and interpreting firms use introductory offers to acquaint new users with their services. A test manual and a coupon redeemable for one computer-generated report can be had for a fraction of what the company usually charges for the service. More recently, some firms have developed software for therapists to use for client interviewing, generation of test reports, and monthly statements. These firms are making substantial use of promotional incentives by offering demonstration diskettes available at nominal cost.

Other professionals have been using sales promotion tools for quite some time. Attorneys have offered initial sessions to prospective clients at very low costs and even gratis for the purpose of discussing whether it would be necessary to continue the relationship. While it may be difficult to think of therapists using introductory offers to attract clients, such tools have already been used ethically and with success. Consider the therapist who offers a workshop on parenting skills, marital enrichment, and the like for a fixed number of sessions at the lower rate than usual is conducting a promotion. The majority of therapists we know who've conducted such workshops, ostensibly for the purpose of delivering only that service, have ended up getting new referrals for treatment. These referrals either come from participants themselves or they are recommended to others. So you see, many therapists have already been using sales promotion and didn't even know it. It's doubtful that even the most conservative among our colleagues would consider the use of workshops for the public an unethical practice.

Another cleaver promotional tool is the information and referral service. This practice promotion technique involves making available information on what services are available, customary fees, where they can be obtained, third party payments, and so on. Information and referral services are frequently operated by practice groups. When it comes time to make a referral for someone who phones, the referral is made to—surprise—one of the members of the practice group. A more sophisticated varient of this approach is to have a series of taped information messages that callers request by number. The equipment used is somewhat expensive but some therapists have found their practice volume grew geometrically within a few months after offering this "service." The information and referral service is not merely a way of generating referrals but also provides a useful and needed public service when built on what Charles Browning (1982) calls the "Seed Principle." His concept is based on the humanitarian notion that in giving one receives. In practice it translates to providing a service whenever possible and when giving the service more than is expected. This makes sense and fits with the value systems of helpers and healers. Strangely enough it is also good advice for people in business. When I (BDF) was growing up my father was in the retail jewelry business. I was required to put in time at the store to learn the business. Many of my uncles were also in the jewelry business and it was a family custom that male children had to learn about the business so they'd have something to "fall back on" just in case they were too inept to do anything else. As luck would have it some of us actually grew up to be lawyers and doctors and such. One of the things that sticks out in my mind is the notion of "good will." I first became acquainted with this concept when I was 15. Someone came in to the store with a knotted up wad of gold chain and asked to have it repaired. I worked at it for about an hour and a half and emerged victorious. I then handed it over to my father who returned it to the customer, smiled, and said "no charge." After the customer left he responded to my poorly concealed annoyance by explaining to me about the importance of building "good will" with people in the community. They could easily shop at a discount store for many of the same items he sold. But the small retailer could provide a little extra service, and might not even charge for it. That's good will, and that, good for business.

Since negative attitudes and demand states often exist for a therapist's services, promotions targeted to referral agents aimed at both educating and persuading can be used. One tool for achieving this end is the promotional letter. One therapist developed a letter she sends to physicians describing services that can be offered to cancer patients and their families. It's reprinted here in its entirety. (See Figure 7)

```
Dear Dr.         ,


         Cancer, stroke, cardiac disease...


As you are well aware, the medical treatment is a significant
part of the prescription but cannot answer all the patient's
needs.  Psychotherapy is often necessary to help the person
and/or his family adjust to the life changes brought on by the
illness and to assist them with planning for the future.

It is often difficult to find a psychotherapist who has had
experience in the health care field and is familiar with and
comfortable in treating pesons suffering from a wide variety of
disorders.  I am a social worker with many years of experience
in medical settings including Lenox Hill Hospital and the Rusk
Institute of Rehabilitation Medicine of New York University
Medical Center.  I have counseled patients with neurological
disorders, cardiac disease, head trauma, spinal cord injury,
and cancer and have also worked extensively with their families.

I am now in private practice and am available to treat patients
and their families who are having a difficult time coping with
the emotional impact of their illness.  At times, this distress
can also affect patient compliance with the medical regimen.
My practice includes crisis intervention and short- and long-
term treatment with individuals ranging in age from adolescents
to geriatrics and with families.

You may refer patients to me directly at the telephone number
found on the enclosed cards.  Please also feel free to consult
with me in advance of a referral.


Sincerely yours,
```

Figure 7

Personal Sales is a person-to-person communication between buyers and sellers (e.g., clients and therapists) or sellers and intermediaries (e.g., therapists and referral agents) and is based on a relationship between the two parties. Most of us have had some experience with personal selling through our contacts with sales clerks in stores and unsolicited telephone calls from people who got our names off of a list. The pushy used car salesman and traveling salesman are the substance of stories and jokes. Such legends evoke a good deal of uncomfortable feelings and the idea of engaging in "selling" strikes a dischordant note in the heart of any self-respecting psychotherapist. Like most stereotypes the one about salespersons is more fantasy than fact, although it is true that most used car salesmen's wardrobes breach the very canons of good taste.

Experts on personal selling, such as Ben Enis, Professor of Marketing at the University of Missouri, contend that sales can be regarded as a profession with its own principles and practice standards (1979) which emphasize an exchange process. There is no doubt that many myths surround the selling occupation much the same as there has been for our own profession. Many people believe that all sales people are extroverted and lack insight. Similarly, there is widespread belief that all psychotherapists are introverted and introspective. We also have had the finger of blame pointed at our manipulativeness much the same as salespersons have. These sweeping generalizations can easily prejudice us so that we may be unwilling to entertain the notion that personal selling might offer some strategies we can use in our practices. Let's consider what is involved in the personal selling process. We can understand personal selling as consisting of five relatively distinct phases: planning, prospecting, presenting, closing, and post-sale servicing.

The planning phase involves the gathering of information on potential buyers, potential referral sources, getting organized for presentations, and generally making sure of the fit between buyer demand and seller desire. Information used in the planning phase ideally will come from the market analysis. The strategy for personal selling should be consistent with overall marketing plans. As we talked about earlier, target segments are selected for specific purposes, and, when personal selling is used, the marketer adjusts her/his approach to fit as nearly as possible with relevant characteristics of the segment based on available information.

The second phase of selling is prospecting, which is the process of getting people to sell to. For therapists, prospects are either referral agents or potential clients. Traditionally, therapists have relied on the method of getting clients through referral rather than directly by making appeals to potential clients. Consequently, the term "prospecting" is one rarely used by therapists but it is one that accurately describes the process. Robert Barker (1984) is the only one, to our knowledge, who uses this term to describe a referral building activity. Instead, we commonly hear about building or cultivating referral sources. This activity is one that is most used by professionals and is accepted practice even among the most conservative lawyers.

Socializing with people who can become or refer clients is so much a part of the culture of professionals that it has become part of our tax code. We can take write-offs for entertaining colleagues with scarcely raising an eyebrow at the IRS. A physician in Texas, we know, deducted the cost of buying and maintaining a rather expensive boat as a professional expense. The IRS looked askant at his return one year and called him in for an audit. When he brought in his calendar and appointment book showing whom he'd taken out on the boat and documented the number of referrals they made to him, his deduction was allowed. Psychologist Bruce J. Schell, Ph.D., claims that whenever he wants to increase his caseload he goes to lunch with a colleague and always gets a referral.

Prospecting that involves socializing is just one of many forms. Because it emphasizes a personal relationship, it epitomises personal selling. Other forms of prospecting are less subtle and seem a lot more like work. Another well known and intensely used prospecting activity is community service. Here, the therapist offers some of her/his time to do volunteer work or consultation at an agency, or serve on their board of directors. Kate Adler, Ph.D., of Kendall, FL, told us that when she was first beginning her practice she volunteered her time at a rape crisis center. As a result, she still gets referrals over ten years later. Doris Stiles, Ph.D., a counseling psychologist in Coral Gables, FL, is a member of several local civic boards which she serves on for the purpose of educating the public regarding specific issues. Although, she is providing a community service and is not serving in the capacity of a psychologist, but a concerned citizen, she ultimately gets referrals from this activity.

Also, giving speeches at PTAs and community service clubs is also a kind of prospecting. Therapists who perform such services are providing a useful public service without a doubt. But at the same time they are building good will for their practice while getting visibility. After all, when someone who attended a speech you gave on child management at the PTA luncheon needs help in managing their own little darling whom do you think they'll call?

In our experience, agencies and service organizations (e.g., Rotary, Jaycees) are constantly on the lookout for new ideas and new people they can call on to make presentations to their membership. Unless you already have a high profile in your community their leadership will not likely know who you are and may very well overlook you. This means that it will be up to you to initiate contact and make your availability known.

One strategy that has been useful is to compile a list of all potential referral sources in your target market and systematically make contact with the leaders. Actually this should be part of your planning. Of course the people or groups you direct your personal sales efforts to will fit with your overall marketing objectives. Some therapists use a variety of strategies for prospecting. One therapist continually scans newspapers and magazines like **Time** and **Newsweek** to get ideas about what is currently in vogue or pop culture. She then uses her findings in speeches that she makes to groups she has identified as most suitable. Most communities have speakers bureaus that you can list yourself with along with those topics you are willing to make presentations on. There are also national speakers bureaus that serve as booking agents for well known personalities, like former presidents and famous authors. Keep them in mind for the future when you actually do become a celebrity.

Some therapists achieve a high profile by virtue of their leisure activities. For many years Edmund Cava, M.D. vigorously pursued his hobby of singing opera. He gained renown throughout Florida as a tenor, performing with the Miami Opera Guild and the Miami Philharmonic, among others. He became known as the "Singing Psychiatrist" and received many referrals as a by-product of his interests.

Another important way of prospecting is associating with other therapists. Amber Goldstein, A.C.S.W., of Coconut Grove, FL, frequently gets referrals from colleagues who are acquainted with her work with phobics. Involvement with professional associations is an activity most of us do as a means of keeping up with new developments and for socialization. Yet, this can be an important source of referrals since we can get visibility among our colleagues. It may be useful to establish relationships with other therapists who have some special expertise in an area you would like to have available for your own clients so that you can make referrals. Then you are in a better position to let your colleages know how you might be able ot help them better serve their clients. We've noticed that non-medical therapists are less inclined to make referrals, preferring to treat almost everyone who walks into their office. In the short run this may be good for their own practice but ultimately can lead to isolation and may limit sources of referrals.

The bane of salespeople is the cold call. This involves getting the name of someone who might be a prospect and either calling on the phone or in person and attempting to make a presentation. The major problem associated with cold calls is that the person being called has not expressed an interest in purchasing the good or service. S/he may not appreciate being contacted and the risk of rejection is extremely high. Technological advances have made it possible for computers to be programmed to make cold calls and telemarketing is enjoying greater use. After all, computers are less sensitive about people hanging up on them. We know of virtually no therapists who make cold calls. As it stands, soliciting clients is considered patently unethical by all professional associations. In the future this may change but will not likely be accepted by therapists for a long time.

Presenting is the next phase of personal selling. For the salesperson with a product to sell this phase involves making a formal presentation and perhaps showing pictures from a catalog or demonstrating how the product works. For a therapist who is giving a lecture this is the time the speech is delivered. Naturally the presentation is suited to audience needs. We all know that talking with a group of business executives requires a different approach than talking to high school students. It is crucial that your presentation be well organized and that you have a professional demeanor void of mannerisms or anything which might distract your audience. For most of them it will be the first — and perhaps only — time you will be seen. The impression you leave could very well determine whether you will ever get a referral. The key to success is to have an interesting topic that you have prepared adequately and make a smooth delivery.

Next is the closing. This is when the order is taken, the contract is signed, the referral is made. Our approach as therapists is usually more subtle than someone with products or other services to sell. We mention closing here to give you the complete picture of the selling process. For anyone wishing to learn more about techniques for closing sales and overcoming objections we recommend Tom Hopkins' *How to Master the Art of Selling* (1982) and Sal Massimino's *How to Master the Art of Closing Sales* (1981). Be forewarned, however, books like these are not for the faint hearted as they are considerably tainted by what you might think of as sleaze and hype. Yet, if you are able to get through some of the possibly offensive material you'll no doubt find that selling emphasizes interpersonal exchange at its simplest level. A buyer has needs and a seller has goods or services. The salesperson's job is to find out what the buyer's needs are and convincingly demonstrate how the goods or services being offered meet these needs. The very nature of the relationship between buyer and seller, much like other relationships, centers on the power to influence. Thus it can easily take on game-like qualities which appear wholly manipulative. To people outside our business, sometimes psychotherapists look pretty much the same.

Finally, personal sales is completed by post-sale service. Most of us have received birthday cards from our life insurance agent and calendars from merchants. These items are designed to let the customer know her/his business is appreciated and to serve as a reminder that the relationship is valued. Very few therapists provide any kind of follow up service to their clients. Perhaps this is an outgrowth of our professional value system. Since we are in the business of confirming and valuing people contacting our clients after we've finished treating them may be an excellent way of reinforcing their progress. One therapists who uses post-sale servicing is Frank MacHovec, Ph.D., of Danville, VA. He sends his clients a small note cared validating their humanity, as shown here as an example.

DIPLOMATE. CLINICAL HYPNOSIS	PHONE: (804) 797-2522

Frank MacHovec PHD ABPH
LICENSED CLINICAL PSYCHOLOGIST

621 MASONIC BUILDING	DANVILLE. VA 24541

THIS CERTIFIES THAT

_____

is a member of the Human Race, having inherent dignity and integrity, with the right to be here and to be happy, to love and be loved, to continually grow into a Better and Better Person.

Figure 8

Contacting a referral agent after receiving a client is extremely important for letting the referral source know that the person s/he referred got there and got treated. Some therapists use printed thank you cards, while others make personal contacts by phone, and still others will send summary letters to referral agents. A noteworthy example of a printed note is the one used by Gil Sandy, M. Div., of Seattle, which is reprinted here. It's probably more important that follow up is done than the form that is used. But it is also worthwhile to pay attention to the most desirable form for follow up as perceived by the referral agents rather than you. Remember, all of your activities should be consistent with your overall marketing plans and a basic position in the market which holds that you are meeting the needs and wants of your clients and referral agents rather than your own.

PUGET COUNSELING CENTER
1111 HARVARD AVENUE
SEATTLE, WASHINGTON 98122

TELEPHONE 329-5050

PLEASE ACCEPT MY THANKS FOR HAVING REFERRED

—————————————————————

TO ME FOR PROFESSIONAL SERVICE

FAMILY CRISIS SERVICE 322-9095

Figure 9

Before leaving the topic of personal sales it is worth mentioning that a significant degree of personal selling occurs while you are conducting therapy. Occasionally we meet a therapist who complains that s/he must work very hard at keeping clients in treatment. In talking with some of these therapists we discover that while they are doing a thorough job of understanding and explaining the dynamics of the clients' problems they are not paying enough attention to the clients. This points to the need for understanding the relationship with the client as more than a part of the treatment context. The relationship a therapist has with a client is also a buyer-seller relationship. Jack Tapp, Ph.D. takes every opportunity he can to educate his clients about the differences between psychiatrists and those psychologists who, like himself, are concerned with health-related behavior. Consequently he gets referrals from his clients. After a session a therapist may expect a client to return for more treatment. This expectation is analogous to the merchant who anticipates repeat business from customers. If the client thinks s/he is getting something that is wanted, a return visit is inevitable. If clients are happy with services they receive from therapists they will refer their friends and family. In my own (BDF) experience satisfied clients have told their physicians about the service they'd received from me and the physician referred other patients. In short, it can be useful to think of all relationships, whether social or business, as having potential for generating referrals. As such, virtually all relationships involve personal selling that can result in opportunities for getting referrals. If you know this you can avoid unsystematic and random interactions which may cost you clients.

Advertising is the paid form of non-personal promotion. Advertising has a lengthy history of bad press among professionals. Actually, the prohibition against advertising began with lawyers a few hundred years ago in England. Back then only the aristocracy was engaged in the profession. The practice of law was regarded as a public duty as opposed to a means of earning a living. Generating income to live on was simply not done by members of this class who relied on their wealth and the land for income. Thus, getting any notoriety to increase business was viewed as being in bad form and was to be carefully avoided since that could lead to lowering the status of the profession to that of an occupation that one toiled over.

Many years later, in 1847 to be precise, concerns within professional associations shifted from creating standards of socially correct behavior to protecting the public when the American Medical Association banned advertising to prevent its members from making blatantly fraudulent and misleading claims for snake oils and other so-called miracle cures. You'll remember these items were very popular during the nineteenth century and there were no government regulations designed to protect consumers. There weren't even laws that prevented little children from working in sweat shops. So, it was incumbent upon the professional associations to act as the conscience of society. These actions were appropriate a few decades ago before labor got organized and prior to big government. But the environment for professional practice has since changed dramatically. We've seen new forms of practice develop such as retail dentistry, walk-in surgery centers, and investor-owned hospitals.

In recognition of the changing environment the United States government stepped in to assure that unrestricted trade could take place. In the mid-1970s two important legal decisions were made. The first was the U.S. Supreme Court decision in 1977 known as Bates v. State Bar of Arizona. This was the famous case which struck down a professional association's restriction against advertising as anti-competitive and an illegal practice which served to unduly restrain trade. Prior to this case ethical codes of most professional associations prohibited advertising and most states included this injunction in licensing laws. How fitting that the legal profession which established prohibitions against advertising initially opened the door for all professions.

In 1979 the Federal Trade Commission ordered the American Medical Association to lift its ban on member advertising. No shrinking violets be they, the AMA, and lawyers were immediately dispatched to fight the FTC. Unfortunately for them, the U.S. Supreme Court agreed with the FTC and upheld the order to stop the AMA from interfering with advertising by members, in a 1982 decision. This decision, as well as a similar case involving the American Dental Association, placed control over advertising under the jurisdiction of the FTC, as opposed to the associations. The FTC places greater emphasis on the legalities of advertising than do associations since it is a regulatory agency. Perhaps it is a mixed blessing that policing of professionals is now going to be the responsibility of a governmental agency and not the profession itself. Whereas a professional association could place sanctions on members for misbehavior, government agencies are empowered to bring criminal charges against a professional for making false or misleading claims. It remains to be seen just what the ramifications of this change will bring. We are inclined to agree with Bloom's (1977) argument that professional associations which were strong enough to stop advertising to begin with are probably strong enough to stop members from conducting deceptive advertising campaigns without the help of government.

When the ban against lawyer advertising was first lifted many people were afraid the air waves and newspapers would be polluted by horrible ads. Although there have been a few ads that breached the canons of acceptable professional demeanor, there has been a good deal less bad advertising than many professionals anticipated. In the health professions, advertising has been much more conservative and probably less used than it might. The professional associations psychotherapists belong to have been less active in modifying their ethical codes for some unknown reasons. Yet, many therapists are comfortable with advertising and, from what we've seen, have kept their ads dignified. Given the trends we've observed for other professions it's doubtful that litigation aimed at changing our associations' formal statements regarding advertising will be necessary, although Overcast, Sales, and Pollard (1982) suggest it is a possibility.

Media used for product advertising have included most conceivable forms, but the greatest concentration has been on television. Advertising on national TV is efficient for goods (e.g., Pepsi-Cola) and services (e.g., Orkin) with national channels of distribution but are not practical for those with local markets. In this case local TV advertising is a better choice. This medium is still relatively underutilized in professional advertising primarily because of the expense associated with its use. Law firms and retail dentists that have used TV ads are those with a sizeable number of practitioners in their operations. Multiple practitioners operating out of a single office is not as common for therapists as for some other professions but is on the rise. The HMO which employs psychotherapists is a practice form that is growing. In addition we are seeing psychologist groups, like the one run by Morton Katz, Ph.D. and Robert Weinberger, Ph.D. in Houston, TX. As this trend continues we expect to see more use made of this medium.

The second most used medium for advertising is newspapers and that is where therapists who advertise have concentrated their efforts. Ads in newspapers fall into two basic categories: **display** and **classified.** Display ads are those you come across while reading news stories and are typically boxed in. Classified ads are usually found in a separate section commonly referred to as "want" ads, but are also found in the news sections as "business directories." Newspaper ads have the advantage over TV by being both cheaper to run and more tangible. Unfortunately they have somewhat less credibility than TV ads which could detract from the impact the ad may have on influencing consumer behavior.

Following TV and newspapers in popularity is direct mail advertising. Most of us have had the experience of opening the mailbox to find it filled with "junk mail" which promptly got pitched in the waste basket. Direct mail advertising has been extremely effective in selling just about everything and continues to be successful. That's why advertisers keep right on stuffing envelopes and mailing them out. Few therapists make use of direct mail for anything more than practice announcements, but the trend is growing. Direct mail can be used as part of a specifically targeted campaign, can be timed, and can be controlled by the advertiser making it an effective medium at a moderate cost. We suggest that you consult the *Direct Mail and Mailorder Handbook* (1974) by Richard Hodgson for more information on direct mail marketing.

Radio ads are also popular for many products and services but have yet to be cultivated by therapists. One of the advantages of radio is that the sales representatives at each station have precise data on exactly who listens to their stations at what times. This simplifies your targeting efforts so that you can create the most suitable message and specify when it is to be aired. Specifying the time an ad is to be aired costs more than leaving it up to the station (known as ROS—run of station) but gives you a better chance of reaching your target group.

Directories are another medium for advertising that have received only modest attention from therapists. When we speak of directories we don't simply mean the yellow pages of the telephone book. This source shouldn't be overlooked, by the way, but don't expect too much. Therapists we talked with who use display ads in the yellow pages have not gotten much success from yellow pages advertising and some even claim that these ads have brought "nuisance" calls from people wanting information only or set an appointment and then fail to show up. Other directories that are available are local business directories, directories of service clubs, chambers of commerce, and professional associations. Directories or guides distributed to newcomers in the community, such as Welcome Wagon, have proven useful to merchants and other service providers; there is no reason why they can't work for you.

Other media for advertising include posters, billboards, signs, car cards (i.e., on buses and subway cars), handbills, and skywriting. Specialty items like T-shirts, pens, calendars, matchbooks, coffee mugs, ashtrays and the like with logos, slogans, or brief messages have been used by many merchants and manufacturers but have been all but overlooked by professionals who advertise. To some this may be a blessing.

There are many opportunities for advertising that exist in the various media but you must remember that your ads should be consistent with your market plans and the image you want to project. It may require some experimenting with messages and media forms along with some reality testing with colleagues before you come up with innovative, tasteful, and effective ads, but hopefully it will become easier in the future as advertising by professionals comes into better repute. We'll talk more about the specifics of creating ads in the next chapter.

Finally, the last type of promotion is **publicity,** which refers to activities that are both non-personal and non-paid. The common forms of publicity are public service announcements and news articles. Broadcast media are owned and operated by private firms for profit. Yet, they are chartered to operate for the best interests of the public. Radio and TV stations are obligated to designate a portion of their time to public service announcements, which take the form of 15, 20, 30 and 60 second spots. Many of the spots are produced by agencies and voluntary organizations, like NIAAA, YWCA, and the American Cancer Society. There is nothing to prevent privately practicing therapists from producing and distributing these announcements and even including a "tag" which identifies them.

Therapists can also get publicity by getting interviewed on radio or television talk shows. Program directors who are constantly on the lookout for new talent and ideas welcome input from professionals in their communities. Robert Mandel, Ph.D., has a weekly television talk show in Columbia, SC. He has become well known in his community and received many referrals as a result. In Miami, FL, Lenoard Haber, Ph.D., has met with similar success but has concentrated his efforts on radio. Somewhat more ambitious is the work of Allen Johnson, Ph.D., of Auburn, MA. He hosts a weekly talk show which is broadcast on cable TV to over 25 cities in central Massachusetts.

Dr. Johnson also manages to write a weekly column for his city newspaper, The *Auburn News*. His column, entitled "Family Focus" includes such titles as "Can Your Children Really Become Video Junkies?" and "Respect is a Mutual Responsibility." Offering to write articles for church, PTA, and other organizational newsletters can also improve the therapist's visibility. Carey Washington, Ph.D., frequently contributes articles on mental health topics to the school newspaper where his daughter is enrolled.

Most newspapers have a section devoted to which local business people got promoted or got elected to offices in their local, state, or national club of association. This resource should not be overlooked as an outlet for information about you. If you publish an article, get board certified, win an award, or develop some innovative treatment you can notify your local paper via a press release so that you can get some publicity for your self and your practice. We'll get into the mechanics of writing a press release in a later chapter.

Giving a speech or conducting a seminar for a group or sponsored by an organization is another way of getting visibility. Not only are you getting publicity but you are also providing a sample of your service. Just to clarify things a bit, earlier we spoke about these activities as personal selling, which they are. But we can also consider delivering a lecture as a form of publicity because the ultimate purpose is to bring yourself and your practice to the attention of potential clients and referral agents. So, in reality, both forms of promotion are contained in this activity.

CHAPTER SUMMARY

The marketing mix is like a recipe of all ingredients and their proportions. For the psychotherapy practice two categories of mix elements can be considered: service features and promotion. Service features consist of **place, price,** and **product,** while promotion is the communication between the therapist and consumers.

Place for a therapist's services involves the geographic location, how clients are referred, the office itself including its decor, and factors connected with availability of the service, convenience, or accessibility. The name used for the practice is also part of place.

Although we often limit our conception of price to the monetary cost of a good or a service, it is more accurate to expand our definition to include all other aspects associated with cost. Missed opportunities, travel and waiting time, physical safety, and psychological discomfort should also be thought of as dimensions of price.

In manufacturing there is little confusion as to what is meant by the term product. Not so in services like psychotherapy. Here, the product includes qualities of the therapist, characteristics of the therapy itself, practice style, and treatment modality.

Promotion is concerned with communicating the most desirable messages to your selected market segments in ways that are both most meaningful and most acceptable **to them.** Promotion is commonly thought of as having four basic "channels": **sales promotion, personal sales, advertising,** and **publicity.**

Sales promotion relies on using incentives to encourage service utilization. These incentives may include introductory offers such as low cost initial consultations or demonstrations to potential clients or referral agents. A recent phenomenon among therapists has been the use of information and referral services by telephone.

Personal sales is based on a realtionship between the referral agent or client and the therapist. Although the term "sales" evokes images of unethical practices, personal sales is the most used promotional tool among all professionals. Social contexts are the major arena for this time honored promotional activity. Interactions between therapist and client during therapy sessions also contain elements of personal selling.

Advertising is both non-personal and paid. Advertising is receiving greater attention in professional service marketing than was formerly true. The impetus for increased advertising by professinals was the 1977 U.S. Supreme Court decision which held that a state bar association's ban on member advertising was an illegal practice which restrained trade. Additional court rulings on medical and dental practitioners' advertising further limited the role professional associations can have in influencing these matters. Despite the increased legal freedom, many therapists hold on to traditional biases against advertising. One psychotherapist made the statement "any therapist who advertises must be a quack." He added, "they make the rest of us look bad and are an embarrassment to the profession."

Publicity is also non-personal, but is non-paid as well. Therapists often provide a public service through this activity. Making public service announcements, preparing news releases, and getting interviewed by members of the press are acceptable to therapists because the publicity they receive helps others besides helping themselves.

CASE EXAMPLES

Parke Fitzhugh received his Ph.D. in clinical psychology in 1970. He's been in full-time private practice since 1980. Until then he held a number of consulting positions with various agencies. Among his interests and specializations is the application of psychology to law enforcement. He became involved with police work while in graduate school when he had an assistantship with a professor who had a grant to work with local police.

As Parke completed his training he was offered the chance to take a position as consulting psychologist with a police department. It was primarily "the nature of the times," as he puts it since there was money available for training officers on how to deal with the public and the desire to apply principles of behavioral science. Initially the responsibilities were limited, but ultimately expanded to include therapy, training hostage negotiators, and assistance in interviewing crime victims. As a part of the demands placed upon him, Parke was required to develop skills in hypnosis. He became fascinated with the subject and developed quite advanced skills.

Through his work with this police department he was asked to consult with a local fire department by the liaison from the county manager's office. Subsequently, other contracts were made with various agencies in the area and he had a pretty busy consulting practice.

Parke believes that these contacts were important but the most important thing for developing his practice has been referrals from clients. He finds that being seen on television, getting interviewed by newspapers, and maintaining a high public profile by serving on boards, being active in the state hypnosis society and county psychological association have been the greatest aids to enhancing his practice. He now divides his time about equally between consulting assignments and traditional private practice.

Jim McKenna has been practicing as a clinical social worker since the early 1960s. The way he first got exposure in the professional community was to hang out a shingle. He was the first social worker in the St. Louis area to do so and at the time, this was almost an act of heresy. He says other social workers were engaging in private practice but they were "doing it on the sly" as there was a general sense that social workers "shouldn't be taking a fee for helping people."

Although he hasn't been active on civic boards, he has been active in the profession. He's a past-president of the Missouri Association for Marriage and Family Therapy and has been active in working on legislation. His notoriety comes more from a willingness to be available and to work out flexible payment plans. In addition, he's been interviewed on both radio and television many times.

Despite his success as an individual therapist who's had a full-time private practice since 1970, Jim has begun using advertising over the past three years now that he's expanded from a solo practice to a group format. He uses 60 second radio spots that advertise the practice rather than any individual. His goal is to provide information about getting treatment. "There are a lot of people who don't have any source of referral and just don't know where to go" he claims. The message to the public is to call for information which is then mailed. Jim makes no efforts to force callers into making an appointment. In fact, he views what he is doing as a service to people. The advertising campaign has resulted in additional clients but he maintains that "we give out more information than appointments."

If he were getting established today or moving in a new direction Jim says that he would study the population he was interested in and "make whatever advertising or whatever public exposure fit the group that needs it." He adds that he'd learn as much as he could about the problem, the referral sources, and get myself known to make my presence felt. Jim knows that "it is all in getting out and getting known."

REFERENCES

Barker, R. L. (1984), *Social work in private practice: Principles, issues, and dilemmas.* Silver Spring, MD: NASW.

Bloom, P. N. (1977), Advertising in the professions: The critical issues. *Journal of Marketing, 44,* 103-110.

Borden, N. H. (1964), The concept of marketing mix. *Journal of Advertising Research, June,* 2-7.

Browning, Charles (1982), *Private practice handbook: The tools, tactics, and techniques for successful practice development.* Los Angeles: Duncliff's International.

Enis, B. N. (1979), *Personal selling: Foundations, process, and management.* Santa Monica: Goodyear.

Hertzberg, D. (1984), Banks are offering no-frills checking to let customers escape increasing fees. *Wall Street Journal,* (8/1/84).

Hodgson, R. S. (1974), *Direct mail and mailorder handbook.* Chicago: The Dartnell Corp.

Hopkins, T. (1982), *How to master the art of selling.* New York: Warner Books.

Kotler, P. (1980) *Marketing management: Analysis, planning, and control.* Englewood Cliffs, NJ: Prentice-Hall.

Levitt, T. (1981), Marketing intangible products and product intangibles. *Harvard Business Review, 59,* 94-102.

MacStravic, R. E. (1977), Marketing health care services: The challenge of primary care. *Health Care Review, 3,* 9-14.

Massimino, S. T. (1981), *How to master the art of closing sales.* New York: AMACOM.

Mone, L. C. (1983), *Private practice: A professional business.* La Jolla, CA: Elm Press.

Overcast, T. D., Sales, B. D. & Pollard, M. D. (1982), Applying antitrust laws to the professions. *American Psychologist, 37,* 517-525.

Trauner, J. B., Luft, H. S., & Robinson, J. O. (1982), *Entrepreneurial trends in health care delivery: The development of retail dentistry and free standing ambulatory services.* U.S. Department of Commerce, National Technical Information Service, P.B. 83-175505.

Thomas, D. R. E. (1978), Strategy is different in service businesses. *Harvard Business Review, 56,* 158-166.

CHAPTER 6

PROMOTION: THE NUTS AND BOLTS

PROMOTIONAL TOOLS like newspaper ads and press releases can be a significant ingredient for running a successful marketing campaign. They are like computer software programs that can be used interchangeably for different purposes. There are many psychotherapists who effectively market their practices without using formal promotions. So, the decision to use certain promotional tools is one you make based on a careful assessment of your market position, your identified segments, your practice goals, and the goals you have in mind for promotion.

Since promotional activities can represent a sizeable outlay of time and money you should consider how you may be able to achieve your goals using each method and evaluate the costs associated with their use. Promotional tools such as advertising have a well-earned reputation for achieving success with almost every kind of venture. This is not to say that any advertising you do will automatically increase your practice because this is far from the truth. Like most activities, promotion is both an art and a science. Many novices have failed to do anything but spend a great deal of money. Bloom (1984) tells an anecdote about a law firm that spent $300,000 in advertising only to go bankrupt. Some professionals have found their promotional materials brought under scrutiny by ethics committees of their professional associations, while others find their reputation among peers to have suffered irreparable damage. But it's not all that bleak. Despite the fact that promotions have risks associated with them, there are also opportunities for increasing revenues and practice volume. The national average for lawyers who actively promote their practices is that for every dollar spent there is an eight dollar return (Baum, 1984). Boulder, Colorado psychologist Michael Shery reports a 960% return on one of his promotional strategies. This means that every dollar he spends generates over nine dollars in practice revenue.

While developing promotional strategies and campaigns is something that is learnable and feasible for you to accomplish, the best advice we can offer you is very simple: go to an expert. Just as personal problem-solving can't always be a do-it-yourself project, neither should promoting your practice. Unfortunately, this advice is almost impossible for any therapist to follow. Why? Primarily because of the bottom line. Advertising agencies are in business to make money. Understandably, the accounts they manage must be large enough to allow them to make a profit. Agencies are given a discount, typically of 15%, by media they place ads in. This amounts to the commission they earn from their clients. If you assume that your ideal annual practice gross is $100,000 and that you follow the general rule of allocating 10% of this budget to marketing, you are left with $10,000 for **all** your marketing efforts.

Now assume that you will spend your entire budget on a newspaper advertising campaign through an ad agency. The agency's total commission is $1500. This is not very much money. Now consider further that, of the agency commission, about 2.2%, or $33, is spent on creative work, or actually writing the copy. It's not very likely that you will get high quality work done by a seasoned copywriter at that price. Benn (1978) suggests a way around this limitation is to pay the agency a creative fee, used specifically for copywriting time, in addition to the regular commission. In this way the budget is only slightly increased and creative work can be maximized. Yet, the figures we've been talking about are undoubtedly much higher than most therapists are willing to spend on marketing; nor do therapists limit their marketing efforts to one kind of media. Thus, the account size of an average therapist for an ad agency is not going to be very large. Some agencies will not even take on accounts that are so small because there is not enough profit in them.

Thus, we offer our second best advice: become an expert yourself. Besides, you still have to take responsibility for deciding on your target segments and the messages you will convey to them. Even if it were feasible for you to hire an agency you must oversee their work and make the final decisions as to what copy is acceptable. If you approach your promotional tasks in a sensible way and are aware of the odds, you should be able to promote your practice effectively. In this chapter we will provide some ideas and general principles that can be used for developing your campaigns. We will also present examples of tools that other therapists have used.

By the time you've gotten up to developing a promotional strategy you've already chosen the service features of your marketing mix. By virtue of these selections you have already determined which elements are to be highlighted in your campaign. Let's consider the steps that you will go through in creating and carrying out your practice promotion.

The first step is for you to decide on the budget that you will allocate for your promotion. Will you spend $200 or $2000 for all of the activities? Then you'll know if you are to be constrained or if you can be extravagent in selecting what is needed to achieve your goals. You then can select the most suitable channels for your promotion. Not all channels are always necessary to get what you want. For instance if you are opening an office for the first time you may decide to use a combination of tools. You may begin with direct mailing (e.g., sending brochures to referral agents), advertising (e.g., placing ads in newspapers announcing your practice), and personal selling (e.g., having an open house for referral agents). Or, if you are using some specific mix of service features to differentiate your practice from other therapists, like moving your practice location closer to a popular shopping mall, might be emphasized in your promotion. In this situation your promotional approach would emphasize this aspect of your practice and you will use a different set of promotional tools to reach your target segment. These might include ads in local newspapers and a publicity campaign.

The next step is for you to devise the message that is most suitable to your selected segments. You already know that different segments will respond to different messages that are communicated in various ways. Yet there are some ground rules that can assist you in preparing the communication. Preparing the message is known as copywriting.

Copywriting can be divided into three parts: the headline, the copy, and the art. There are several suggestions we've gleaned from successful advertising and marketing experts we want to share with you. Probably the most important bit of information is that clever and creative copy is unnecessary and may even work against you. In other words, the message itself is more important than how it is said. This is true provided the message is stated clearly and succinctly and applies equally to headlines and copy. Everyday language free of both ambiguity and jargon is best. The goal is to develop material that gets across what you want communicated. Simple seems to work best in getting across the message. You are not trying to impress anyone with cute sayings or clever poetry. Advertising moguls like David Ogilvy (1982) and John Caples (1974) caution us that creative copy might win awards but by and large it is not the award winning copy that does the job of getting responses or making sales. A brochure or newspaper ad that shows the headline "TENSION" in large letters with the statement "Relieved by Dr. Smith. Call 987-1234" underneath may seem creative. Unfortunately it is ambiguous. A simpler presentation which appeals to a reader's self-interest and provides an explanation of Dr. Smith's services will be more effective in 1) getting read, 2) being understood, and 3) bringing in clients.

There are some other rules of thumb to keep in mind. For example, headlines that offer a benefit or appeal to a consumer's needs or interests are more likely to be read than headlines that make no promise. If there is no perceived benefit, the rest of the copy may not even be read. Caples (1974) suggests that the next best kind of headline is the one that gives news, followed by one that arouses curiosity. In practical terms this rule can be put into effect with headlines like this.

NOW YOU CAN LEARN TO RELAX

This headline is designed to get the reader's interest piqued so s/he wants to read the copy to find out how to relax. A headline for the same service that is presented as news might be phrased

NOW AVAILABLE: THE LATEST TECHNIQUES FOR RELAXING

Someone who may already know how to relax may be interested in finding out other ways and get into the copy to get more information. Similarly, a potential client who has been unsuccessful in learning relaxation skills may think s/he can be helped by another method or perhaps another therapist who knows some different techniques than past therapists. A headline that arouses the reader's curiosity might be stated as

HOW I LEARNED TO BECOME RELAXED IN JUST ONE WEEK

Headlines that use both product or service name as well as state price tend to be read and bring in better responses than those leaving such information out. A headline that has these qualities may be one like

LEARN THE NEWEST WAYS TO RELAX FROM DR. SMITH FOR JUST $25

Headlines that include date or time limitations are useful in getting readers to respond to copy. For example

LEARN TO RELAX BEFORE SCHOOL BEGINS

might be run for a month before the school year begins.

Ads for introductory offers are good at getting readers into copy since they appeal to a reader's wish for a bargain.

LEARN THE ART OF RELAXING FOR 1/2 THE REGULAR COST

or

WANT TO LEARN TO RELAX? FREE CONSULTATION

Some other important points about headlines should also be kept in mind. Photographs or illustrations can be helpful if they are relevant to your headline and copy. Unfortunately, illustrations that are immediately meaningful to you may be misunderstood by others. If they are, the reader can easily get confused, and a confused reader will not become a consumer. If you use illustrations, line drawings re-produce better than photographs and usually at less cost, particularly in newspapers. Also, a short headline is generally better than a long one. But if you have a message to convey and it's fairly long, go ahead and use it anyway. Otherwise you run the risk of not having your message understood and the reader will not get into the copy. Avoid bragging and boasting. Not only does this detract from your ethical and professional stature, it is ineffective for getting reader response.

There are some other pieces of general advice that apply to copywriting. For instance, long copy sells better than short copy. Once a consumer begins to read, watch, and/or listen there is greater opportunity for your message to be conveyed if the copy is long. Since the purpose of the headline is to get readers to read the rest of the copy, think in terms of motivating interest to get into the copy. If you use long copy in print break it up with sub-headings, known in the trade as cross heads, which allow a reader who skims to get your basic message in telegraph fashion.

Another useful bit of advice is to keep your writing simple by using concrete words in familiar language, the kind your reader is likely to encounter every day. It's not that you are assuming the reader is too stupid to understand what you're saying or too lazy to work at it. On the contrary, you are showing respect by meeting her/him where s/he is psychologically. You already know that when you do this with a client in a therapy session it contributes to building rapport. To get even further comfort on the reader's part be sure to talk directly to the reader as if s/he is an individual you are speaking with in person. Most people read while they are alone so using the word "you" will seem appropriately personal.

Appealing to a reader's self interest increases the chance that they will act on what they've read. People are motivated by two things: getting what they want and avoiding getting something that they don't want. If you understand your target segment in sufficient depth, figuring out an appeal should be relatively easy.

People also respond to testimonials. The use of testimonials by professionals has not been an acceptable practice since it does not convey the kind of demeanor that is consistent with professional ethical standards. So, you should probably stay away from using testimonials from satisfied clients unless you can work out some ways of making them tasteful and that conform to ethical standards. One of the interesting findings from the advertising research literature is that TV ads that used testimonials from celebrities were remembered by viewers, but **what** was being advertised was not. This was also true for ads that were very entertaining. Yet, testimonials from persons designated as experts were persuasive and the products were remembered by viewers. So, an ad featuring a famous athlete who endorses a running shoe is going to have more credibility than the same ad with Orson Welles. The value of these findings for you is that if you really want to use a testimonial in your promotion you might think about emphasizing the merit of your work by someone with the status of an expert. For example, if you work with children your ad might feature a teacher's endorsement.

Printed design and format are also important considerations. Copy that appears to emulate news has proven to work well repeatedly for both print and broadcast media. Lettering should be primarily lower case and should be of a type size and style that is customarily encountered by the reader. Using all caps or extreme type sizes should be limited or used sparingly for special effect. The constrast between print and background should make the reader comfortable otherwise s/he will stop reading. For brochures and newspaper ads black on white works fine as do other soft colored backgrounds like buff and yellow. White print on a black background should be avoided altogether as should any arrangement that makes it difficult for the reader, like unusual shaped paragraphs. If there's going to be a struggle you'll come up the loser because a reader will not spend time with any copy that's not easy to read.

Timing is also an important consideration. A promotional campaign that is well planned but gets overshadowed by a significant news event or a seasonal occurrence can fall flat on its face. Successful professional service marketing expert Jay Schlaks learned about timing the hard way. He said "running ads around major holidays is just a waste of money."

"People are too busy with themselves and their families to pay any attention to you" he added. Since one aim of promoting your practice is to gain recognition of your availability, frequency of exposure is more important than the size of your layout. Large layouts are striking and can be very expensive. But according to David Ogilvy (1982) you'd be better off spending the same amount of money (or less!) on repetition. If you are using effective copy you'll enjoy a good return on your investment. When preparing copy it can be helpful to ask yourself whether this material can be used for the next 20 years. You've probably noticed ads on TV and in magazines that have changed little over the years. Pay attention and learn from them, because they contain copy that works. If they weren't effective they would have been scrapped long ago.

The next step is for the promotional efforts to be carried out. Mail the brochures, run the ads, and so forth. Your plan is implemented so you can presumably reap the rewards of your labors. Then you'll be able to proceed to the next step which is to evaluate what you've accomplished besides spending a good deal of energy and money. Advertising and marketing experts are in accord that your promotional efforts should always be evaluated. Never rely on opinions; always use data advises John Caples (1974). "I've had clients spend $50,000 on ads in a six month period and I can tell you exactly which ones have worked" says Jay Schlaks. There is no formula for making successful promotional materials. What works in one market may not work in another market. By the same token, one segment's positive response is no indicator of the response another will have. The only way to know for certain is to test your materials.

Based on the results you get you may have to revise your materials. Then you go through the same process of redesigning and retesting your materials. It's a cycle that continues and allows for self-correction. It's important to test and revise periodically because market conditions are subject to change.

Now let's examine the different channels within each promotional category more closely and look at some examples therapists have used in their practices.

Sales Promotion

There are several categories of sales promotion tools. Among them are brochures, sales letters, client information handouts, newsletters, and coupons. Easily the most common promotional tool used by therapists has been the brochure. Brochures are accepted as a means of communicating with prospective clients and referral agents because of their educational and informational flavor. Many therapists overlook brochures as anything but an expense they can do without. This is a mistake. Although brochures provide a variety of facts that can assist someone in making a decision concerning a referral they are invaluable in emphasizing a service feature that you have built into your practice. In this connection they can serve as a mini-commercial for one or more service features for your practice, and for you. No one will ever accuse you of being unethical if you prepare brochures for your practice, as long as they stay within the confines of professional ethics.

Grover Loughmiller, Ph.D., of Tyler, TX uses computerized assessment in his practice. This service feature is emphasized in a brochure that is distributed to potential clients. In it this service is explained and fee information is provided. In addition, other therapeutic and consulting services that are available from Dr. Loughmiller and his associates are described.

Drs. Gertrude and Kingsley Montgomery of Birmingham, MI run a group practice offering a comprehensive array of services. A promotional tool they use is a no-cost information service that is accessed over the telephone. A caller simply requests a tape on a desired topic by number and listens to a pre-recorded message. To let people know about this free service the Montgomery's distribute a brochure. They provide additional information about their other services and also highlight a service feature that differentiates them from other providers: they've been in their town longer than any other psychologist group.

Danny Wright is a social worker in Amarillo, TX, specializing in marriage and family therapy. He uses his brochure to educate potential consumers about the specialty so that clients or referral agents wanting a therapist who thinks about adjustment problems as relationship-focused will know where to turn for assistance.

Anne Gottlieb Angerman, M.S.S.W., of Aurora, CO uses her brochure to call attention to her special approach to treatment. Her cover repeats the phrase "a new concept in counseling" several times in type that is arranged diagonally, which is effective in catching a reader's attention yet is easily read. Then she explains what is unique about her as a therapist and the way she works. She also further differentiates herself, as a woman, who in her opinion, is better able than a male therapist to treat another woman.

Dr. Windy Dryden of Birmingham, England uses his brochure to emphasize his skills in Rational Emotive Therapy and the ways in which he qualified to treat people. His brochure is unusual because he includes a testimonial from Albert Ellis, the orignator of Rational Emotive Therapy, who comments on Dr. Dryden's achievements.

The Life Counseling Center is a practice group in southern New Jersey. They use a brochure to inform clients about their mix of sevice features which includes availability seven days a week, a complete line of treatment services, and multiple locations. This willingness to flex fees is also mentioned.

Another frequently used tool is the client-handout. Frank MacHovec, Ph.D. of Danville, VA likes to use a leaflet to let his clients know about his fees, confidentiality, and the kinds of services he offers. He also takes this opportunity to describe his special training and makes a brief autobiographical presentation which bolsters his credibility. He says he actually spends very little money on these materials because he has them mimeographed. The client handout J. Davis Mannino, M.S.W. of San Francisco, spells out in detail qualities of the client-therapist relationship and his policy regarding fees. He points out to his clients that he welcomes referrals and is willing to offer a complimentary session to anyone who a client refers, which is a form of sales promotion.

Also of value as a promotional device are materials you send to your clients. Every month when Allen Hedberg, Ph.D., of Fresno, CA sends out his bills, he encloses a one page mental health note reprinted on his letterhead. These are nice because they take a little of the sting out of receiving a bill and they convey a message of caring. Psychologist Susan Sturdivant of Dallas, TX got the idea that sending a newsletter to clients would help them by providing useful information. She was right and her clients appreciated her efforts so well that her practice volume increased 30%. Because she has an interest in writing she decided to devote more energy to creating newsletters containing a variety of topics which can be purchased from her at a reasonable cost. If you like, she'll even customize them with information about you. For details about these newsletters contact Susan Sturdivant, Ph.D., 5307 East Mockingbird, Suite 401, Dallas, TX 75206.

A promotional mailing for business in West Jordan, Utah included discount coupons for both counseling and educational classes at the Jordan Valley Counseling Clinic with V. G. Smith, Jr., D.S.W. Coupons such as these are classic sales promotion tools which are new for psychotherapists.

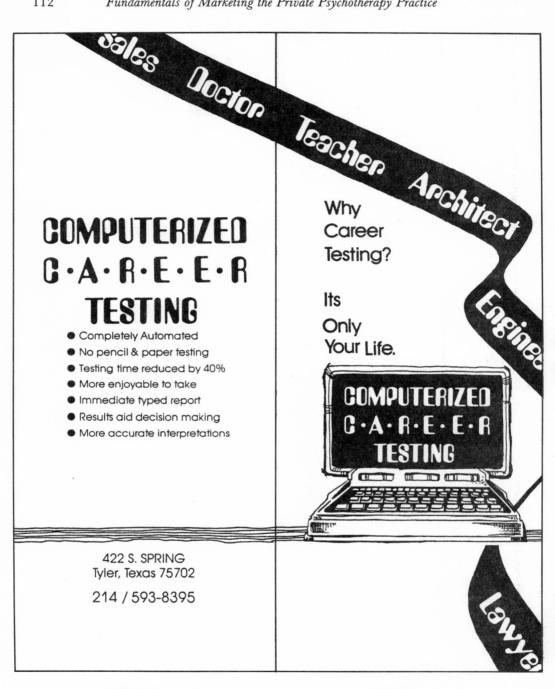

pamphlet back - page 4   pamphlet front - page 1

Figure 10

Recent studies estimate 25% of all U.S. workers (24 million) are unhappy in their jobs, and that 10 years after college, 75% of all graduates are not in jobs for which they were prepared! Will you be one of these?

Testing & Evaluation Services

You are provided the most up-to-date and comprehensive career assessment service available, tailored by our staff to meet your individual needs. The detailed assessment includes an in-depth look at your:

- Vocational Interests
- Intellectual Abilities
- Job-Related Personality Traits

All testing is done on a computer console and a printed evaluation of the results is provided immediately upon test completion. The report contains:

- List of Recommended Occupations
- Complete and Easy-To-Read Explanation of Results
- Graphic Profile of Interests, Abilities and Personality Traits
- Summary of Results

After test completion you will review the report with a staff member, who will assist you in making future plans.

Additional Services:

Complete Psychological Testing and Evaluation
Personal, Family and Marriage Counseling
Weight Loss and Habit Control
Time and Stress Management
Employee Assistance Programs
Management and Educational Consulting

For More Information:

THE LOUGHMILLER INSTITUTE FOR HUMAN BETTERMENT

(214) 593-8395

422 S. Spring   Tyler, Tx. 75702

Who can be Tested?

Anyone age 13 or older who is:

- Undecided about a career or college-major
- Interested in changing careers, or exploring new career options
- Re-entering the job market after some absence
- Feeling dissatisfied with their present career

What is the Cost?

The typical assessment **and** consultation fee range is $125.00 to $400.00, depending on the type and number of tests desired. Where appropriate, testing without consultation may be provided.

How Much Time is Involved?

Actual testing time is usually one to three hours, and one to two hours of consultation time is needed with a staff member. The assessment can be done in one day or divided to fit your schedule. Weekday, evening and Saturday appointments are available.

COMPUTERIZED C·A·R·E·E·R TESTING

Staff:

John C. Hopkins, M.S. — Counseling Associate with extensive experience in high school and college student counseling.

Grover C. Loughmiller, PhD. — Director and Consulting Psychologist in private practice for over 11 years.

Jacqueline Nolin, PhD. — Computer Services Coordinator and Administrative Associate.

pamphlet - page 2   pamphlet - page 3

Figure 10 (*continued*)

DO YOU HAVE QUESTIONS ? ? ?

. . . ABOUT YOUR FEELINGS

. . . ABOUT YOUR PROBLEMS

NOW YOU CAN RECEIVE

PSYCHOLOGICAL HEALTH

INFORMATION . . . .

BY JUST DIALING YOUR

TELEPHONE . . . . .

AND LISTENING . . .

For the "Psychological Health Tape Information Service" . . .

. . . simply dial 642-9080 and request the tape number of your choice:

1.   Self-Confidence & Self Esteem

2.   Teenage Problems

3.   What is a Clinical Psychologist?

4.   Divorce & Rejection

5.   Sleep Problems

6.   Obesity & Permanent Weight Control

7.   Fears & Phobias

8.   Impotence

9.   Alcohol Problems

10. Relationship Problems Marital & Others

11. Premature Ejaculation

12. Problems with Female Orgasm

13. Managing Stress Successfully

14. When to Consider Phychological Help

15. Anxiety

16. Depression

Figure 11

This "Psychological Health Tape Information Service"
. . .

. . . is a public service offered by:

** MONTGOMERY & ASSOCIATES **

Outpatient Clinic

Personal Growth Center

690 East Maple Road
Birmingham, Michigan 48011

Telephones: 642-8042

642-1211

* * * * * * * * * * *

The Tape Information Service

is free of charge to the

caller.

* * * * * *

Let us know if you like it .

. . . and if it is helpful

to you.

MONTGOMERY & ASSOCIATES

. Located in Birmingham
  for 19 years . . . oldest
  Psychologist Service
  group

. Offers seminars, group
  consultation on helping
  people to cope with their
  concerns and special needs

. Offers Support Groups

. Blue Cross approved, as
  well as other insurance

. Certified to counsel:

  . Marriage
  . Divorce
  . Pre-marital
  . Problems of aging
  . Family
  . Parent effectiveness
  . Pregnancy/Aborton
  . Adolescent
  . Child
  . Learning disability
  . Sexual adjustment
  . Interpersonal problems
  . Ego identity
  . Delinquency
  . Vocational

MONTGOMERY & ASSOCIATES

Outpatient Clinic

Personal Growth Center

690 East Maple Road
Birmingham, Michigan 48011
PHONES: 642-8042 - 642-1211

Figure 11 *(continued)*

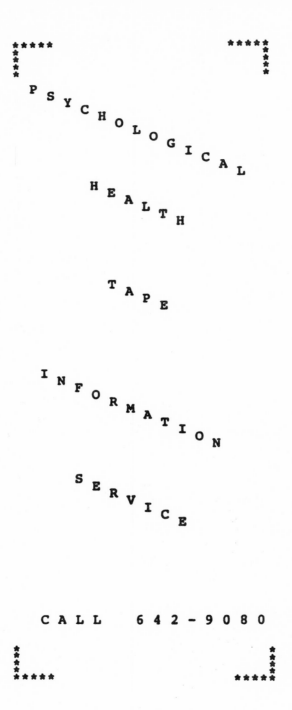

Figure 11 *(continued)*

Personal Counseling

Marriage and Family Therapy

Pre-Marital Therapy

Divorce Counseling

Group and Individual Psychotherapy

Parent-Child Counseling

Consultation

Danny Wright, M.S.S.W.

Figure 12

Many emotional or behavioral problems arise in families and marriages, and are often expressions of troubled relationships. Physicians, clergymen, educators, and other professionals frequently encounter such problems, but may not be in a position to respond to them effectively.

The professional specialization of Marriage and Family Therapy focuses on troubled human relationships, whether they are manifested in marital or sexual dysfunction, parent-child problems, or individual symptoms of psychological maladjustment.

Marriage and Family Therapists, who are trained as traditional psychotherapists before specializing in Marriage and Family Therapy, approach such problems using a variety of techniques, which may include group, couple, family or individual psychotherapy, premarital or divorce therapy, sex therapy, or hypnotherapy.

Figure 12 *(continued)*

Marriage and Family Therapists are certified by the American Association for Marriage and Family Therapy, or the American Family Therapy Association. They may also maintain other professional affiliations by virtue of training in such fields as counseling or social work.

Consultation, requests for more information, or referrals for Marriage and Family Therapy are invited:

> Danny Wright, M.S.S.W.
>
> 5410 B. Bell
>
> Amarillo, Texas 79109
>
> 806/352-0527

American Association for Marriage and Family Therapy

Certified Social Worker - Advanced Clinical Practitioner

Licensed Professional Counselor

National Association of Social Workers

Academy of Certified Social Workers

Figure 12 *(continued)*

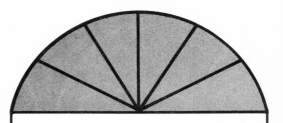

A NEW CONCEPT IN COUNSEL-
ING • A NEW CONCEPT IN
COUNSELING • A NEW CON-
CEPT IN COUNSELING • A
NEW CONCEPT IN COUNSELING

PURPOSE

This pamphlet will tell you about my practice of social work and also give you a useful insight into what occurs during counseling.

ABOUT YOUR COUNSELOR

After graduating from the University of Wisconsin in 1973 with a Masters Degree in Social Work and Rehabilitation Counseling, Ms. Angerman worked in various public Mental Health Centers and was later affiliated with a large community hospital, where she gained extensive experience in both individual and group counseling. She is certified in the State of Colorado as a licensed Social Worker.

In 1981, she started a private practice of Clinical Social Work. Her office is located within a medical suite of Family Practice physicians, providing a comfortable setting in which to serve patients with a variety of social, emotional, reproductive, sexual, and psychosomatic problems.

In addition to counseling, Ms. Angerman lectures and conducts workshops in communications, assertiveness, women's concerns, parenting, and stress management.

Q *How Does A Clinical Social Worker Differ From A Psychiatrist Or Psychologist?*

A Mainly in training. A Psychiatrist has a degree in medicine, can prescribe medication and can admit patients to a hospital for treatment.

The training of a Social Worker or Psychologist is derived from more academic sources, with emphasis on the social sciences. To practice, a Psychologist must have a Doctorate in Psychology whereas a Social Worker may practice with a Masters Degree. All three professionals can do "psychotherapy", and have extensive training in working with individuals, couples, families, and groups.

Q *Why Should I See A Social Worker?*

1421 S. Potomac
Suite 330
Aurora, CO 80012
Office (303) 696-0472
Home (303) 750-6402

Stress Management and Relationship Counseling

Anne Gottlieb Angerman
M.S.S.W., L.S.W.II

Figure 13

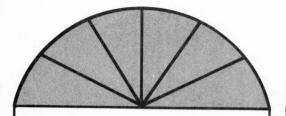

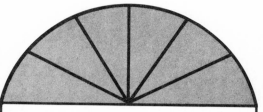

A It has only been since 1976 that Social Workers have been licensed in Colorado to practice psychotherapy. Therefore, many people are not aware of the broad range of services that may be performed by a Social Worker, and are frequently confused by the stereotype of Social Workers as "those who work with people on welfare". Generally, the professional services of a licensed Social Worker are less costly then comparable counseling services of a Psychologist or Psychiatrist.

Q *When Should A Person Seek Help?*

A The best time to make an appointment with a qualified professional is when a person is not feeling good about what is going on in his or her life, or is experiencing fear, anger, depression, or anxiety that interferes with daily activities over a period of time. Another clue to the need for counseling may be a problem that never seems to get resolved, or feeling that certain relationships are causing undue conflict, tension, and pain. It is better to seek counseling before a true crisis arises; however, it is sometimes the crisis itself that motivates a person to seek help, such as the death of a loved one, being fired from a job, or feeling rejected in a relationship.

Sandy L. came to see me after she and her boyfriend broke up a month earlier. She could not function on her job and was experiencing insomnia. In the course of her counseling, she came to realize she was still very angry at her ex-boyfriend and also was not feeling good about their earlier interactions.

Q *What Happens In The First Session?*

A After obtaining preliminary background information, your Therapist will seek to identify the true nature and extent of the problem. Sometimes what seems to be the problem may only be a symptom of a larger problem. Then, you will be given a clear assessment of the situation. As the Therapist discusses the kind of plan that will most effectively support you in solving your problem, along with appropriate cost and scheduling considerations, you will have an opportunity to determine if you want to continue working together.

Q *What is The Difference Between Psychoanalysis And Psychotherapy?*

A Psychoanalysis is a type of treatment that can only be done by a Psychiatrist. It is extremely intensive with three or more appointments each week, focusing on past and unconscious behavior. Typically, the patient lies on a couch and has minimal eye contact with the Therapist.

In comparison, Psychotherapy tends to be more reality oriented dealing with issues which affect your life and lifestyle, as well as certain influences from your past. During a typical session, the patient sits comfortably in a chair facing the Therapist. The environment is professional; yet warm and friendly. The conversation is direct and to the point; issues are examined objectively and honestly.

Q *How Many Appointments Will I Need?*

A It varies from patient to patient and from problem to problem. After the first two sessions your Therapist will be able to estimate the number of appointments you may need to effectively resolve the present situation. Generally, appointments are made on a weekly basis.

Q *What May I Expect To Achieve From Counseling?*

A Most patients would agree they achieve more insight and awareness about themselves. Counseling is an opportunity to explore feelings and to understand why you do certain things, especially behavior that can be self-destructive to yourself or to others. It is also an opportunity to "look at" and evaluate present relationships and to determine if changes are appropriate. In short, therapy can be considered a type of "self-enrichment".

Sometimes you might be asked to read a certain book or to experiment with different behavior techniques, such as assertiveness.

Hopefully, as time goes on, you will feel better about yourself, and have more confidence in yourself through increased awareness of who you are.

Figure 13 *(continued)*

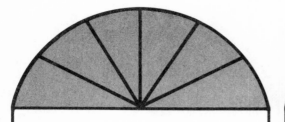

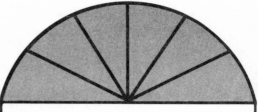

Q *Should My Spouse Or Any Other Family Member Have Counseling, Too?*

A When the problem involves another person, such as a spouse or children, it is often advisable for them to participate in the therapy. Naturally, they must be willing to do so, and to share your commitment in finding new solutions to old problems.

Q *Why Are Some People Afraid Of Seeking Help?*

A Many times, people don't seek help because they feel they don't need it. Others are simply afraid to find out about themselves. There is still the connotation that seeking help is like admitting to being crazy. Quite to the contrary--seeking help often means looking at yourself and facing up to yourself.

Q *What Are Some Symptoms That Suggest The Need For Professional Help?*

A These symptoms include insomnia, psychosomatic problems, weight problems, unhappiness, or the inability to sustain a relationship or a job.

Sharon L. could not eat at mealtimes. She cried a lot, couldn't concentrate on anything, and had no interest in her appearance. Her physician was concerned about her well-being and referred her to a Social Worker. She was suffering from depression and her symptoms began shortly after she was terminated from her job. She suddenly felt very afraid and very threatened, and was unable to express her anger about recent events in her life.

Psychosomatic problems often are experienced by persons when they are having stress. Some of these conditions are: diarrhea, ulcers, eating problems, and head and back problems.

Q *What Is Stress Management And Relationship Counseling?*

A Stress management is the process of learning to recognize stress in your life and then finding ways to deal with it. Stress can be dealt with effectively through counseling, proper nutrition, exercise, and new activities. Stress management also involves learning ways to prevent or reduce stress in your life. Stress can be caused by any number of factors, such as on-going job and financial pressures, and not having enough time for oneself. Especially with more women working, increased stress is noted because of heavier demands at home and conflicts associated with sharing more responsibilities.

Liz J. came to realize how she chose men that were unsuitable for her and why they would not give her a commitment. Yet, this was what she really wanted.

Relationship counseling is the process of looking at close relationships, learning what causes problems in them, and finding new techniques to deal with problem areas more effectively. It also involves realizing how much changing can be done by all parties involved, or accepting the relationship.

Q *Is It Better For A Woman To See A Woman Counselor?*

A Each person has their own preference. However, studies have shown that women feel more comfortable talking to other women. In general, more women tend to present themselves more for counseling than men.

Figure 13 (continued)

W. DRYDEN BSc, DipCouns, MSc, PhD, ABPsS
Counselling Psychologist

209 Belchers Lane,
Little Bromwich,
Birmingham B9 5RT
021 772 7948

Psychotherapy & Counselling Services

A PRIVATE REFERRAL SERVICE

Referrals will be welcomed

for the following psychological problems:

- Anxiety and Stress

- Phobias

- Psycho-sexual problems

- Relationship and marital problems

- Depression and low confidence

- Eating and smoking problems

- Work-related problems

- Underachievement

- Life crisis problems
  — Bereavement
  — Redundancy
  — Divorce
  — Serious illness

Figure 14

DR. W. DRYDEN is a nationally known counselling psychologist who has had over ten years experience in the fields of counselling and psychotherapy in Britain and the United States of America His ACCOMPLISHMENTS include:

- Providing effective counselling and psychotherapy services in a general practice setting — over five years experience.
- Counselling distressed individuals and couples in educational and marriage guidance settings.
- Training over 250 counsellors, psychologists and psychotherapists in psychological counselling and the cognitive therapies.
- Organizing and co-ordinating teaching on the postgraduate diploma in counselling course at Aston University.
- Organizing and co-ordinating counselling services at the University Counselling Service at Aston University.
- Writing over 40 published articles on developments in counselling and psychotherapy.
- Founding and editing the "British Journal of Cognitive Psychotherapy."
- Editing books on counselling and psychotherapy including "Individual Therapy in Britain" and "Marital Therapy in Britain. Volumes 1 and 2" — all published by Harper and Row.

He is the leading exponent of Rational-Emotive Therapy in Britain and is the author of "Rational-Emotive Therapy: Fundamentals and Innovations." London: Croom-Helm, 1984.

RATIONAL-EMOTIVE THERAPY places great emphasis on the interrelationship of thinking, behaviour and emotions. It is based on the concept that anxiety, hostility, guilt and depression stem from self-defeating attitudes and beliefs currently held by the individual, and from faulty social learning experiences. By learning to alter the beliefs which help create their upsetting emotions, people can develop greater capacities for dealing with their current problems, and live freer and more emotionally satisfying lives.

Figure 14 *(continued)*

Testimonial from Dr. Albert Ellis, the founder of Rational-Emotive Therapy and one of the world's most influential psychotherapists:

Institute for Rational-Emotive Therapy

45 East 65th Street, New York, New York 10021 (212) 535-0822

To Whom it May Concern:

September 29, 1983

This is to note that I have known Dr. Windy Dryden for the last six years and have been in steady touch with him, through correspondence and through personal contact, during that time. I have supervised a good deal of his work in rational-emotive therapy and have had him work with me as an associate therapist in some of my regular therapy groups.

In the course of my working with Dr. Dryden I have always found him to be an exceptionally intelligent and competent counseling psychologist and psychotherapist. He has an unusually fine grasp of rational-emotive therapy (RET) and has made some original contributions to its theory and its practice. He has a most sincere interest in people and gets along beautifully with his clients and with other professionals. I think that he is unquestionably the outstanding practitioner of RET in the British Isles and that there are few as competent as he is in this respect in the entire world. In addition to his clinical work, his writing is clear, precise, and highly readable and I feel sure that he will become increasingly known throughout Britain and throughout the world for his contributions in this area.

On the basis of my first-hand experience with Dr. Dryden I can unhesitatingly recommend him as a psychologist, as a psychotherapist, and as a scholar and I can think of virtually no position in the field of psychology which he could not most ably fill.

Sincerely yours,

Albert Ellis, Ph.D.
Executive Director

AE:wd

A non profit community agency chartered by the Regents of the University of the State of New York

Figure 14 *(continued)*

SERVICES in:

Counselling

Individual Therapy

Marital/Couple Therapy

Group Therapy

Stress Management

Sex Therapy

Figure 14 *(continued)*

The Life Counseling Center, P.A.

386 W. State Hwy. No. 70, **Marlton**, NJ 08053 ⟩ **(783-2322)**
13 East Laurel Road, **Stratford**, NJ 08084
321 Shore Road, **Somers Point**, NJ 08244 ⟩ **(625-2062)**
Rt. 50, **Mays Landing**, NJ 08330

> BULK RATE
> U.S. POSTAGE
> **PAID**
> CHERRY HILL, NJ 08034
> PERMIT NO. 806

pamphlet outside front

 The Life Counseling Center, P.A.

Since its beginning in 1978, The Life Counseling Center has been dedicated to providing a broad spectrum of high quality mental health services to the Southern New Jersey Community. We began with the idea that individuals and families should be able to find the counseling or support services they need "under one roof" and at a reasonable cost. Today we have a staff of psychologists, marriage and family therapists, and certified alcoholism counselors available 7 days a week and evenings at four convenient locations.

Here are the Special Services we offer:

* **MARRIAGE** — practical counseling aimed at providing concrete ways by which men and women may live together with excitement, cohesiveness and intimacy.

* **FAMILY** — counseling sessions with the entire family. Focus on living together with unity.

* **CAREER AND EMPLOYMENT** — provides career interest assessment, productive resumes, job interview skills, career/job direction, new confidence.

* **DEPRESSION, STRESS, ANXIETY & RELATION-SHIP DIFFICULTIES** — traditional therapy and hypnosis to assist individuals in coping with the stresses of life and the accompanying emotional ups and downs.

* **ALCOHOL, GAMBLING, & DRUG PROBLEMS** — individual and group counseling with practical, daily treatment plans.

* **SCHOOL** — counseling for children and adolescents. Special attention to behavior, motivation, achievement, social and learning disability programs.

* **INFERTILITY & ADOPTION** — specialized counseling to help couples cope and explore new options.

* **PSYCHOLOGICAL TESTING** — administered by licensed psychologists as a tool in diagnosing and treating emotional difficulties and learning problems. Neuropsychological testing aids in the diagnosis and treatment of learning disabilities.

FEES: Based on the ability to pay for services. Most insurance plans reimburse for psychological services.
TO RECEIVE HELP: Call for an appointment at any time. There is no waiting list.

OFFICES LOCATED AT:
386 W. State Hwy. No. 70, **Marlton**, NJ   783-2322
13 East Laurel Rd., **Stratford**, NJ   783-2322
321 Shore Road, **Somers Point**, NJ   625-2062
Route 50, **Mays Landing**, NJ   625-2062

Bruce A. Naylor, Ph.D. - Executive Director
New Jersey License #1446
Jay Schmulowitz, Ph.D. - Clinical Director
New Jersey License #1234
Licensed Psychologists
Denise Bucich-Naylor, Ph.D. - Director of Training
Geoffrey D. Nusbaum, Ph.D. - Director of Development

pamphlet inside

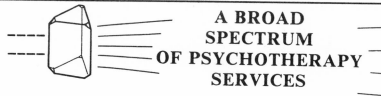

A BROAD SPECTRUM OF PSYCHOTHERAPY SERVICES

 The Life Counseling Center, P.A.

pamphlet outside back

Figure 15

C O N S U M E R

A W A R E N E S S

I N F O R M A T I O N

... to help you

evaluate needs

and compare

alternative

treatments ...

Frank MacHovec PhD
Licensed Clinical Psychologist
145 Marshall Terrace
Danville, Virginia 24541

PHONE: 804-797-2522

Figure 16

SERVICES PROVIDED

Individual, group, family, marital, divorce, and sex therapies; hypnotherapy for habit control, pain relief, phobic desensitization, and consultation services to business, community agencies, and to the legal profession.

TREATMENT SPECIALIZATION

Dr. MacHovec provides a blend of treatment methods which include but are not limited to psychoanalytic, neoanalytic, Gestalt, cognitive-behavioral, transactional analysis theories and practices in a basically phenomenological-existential milieu.

QUALIFICATIONS

Dr. MacHovec is a Licensed Clinical Psychologist in Virginia and a Licensed Practicing Psychologist in North Carolina. He has B.A., M.A., and Ph.D degrees in psychology with a one-year pre-PhD and two years post-PhD full-time internships in mental hospitals in Alaska and Idaho. He was awarded a Diplomate in Clinical Hypnosis in 1981 by the American Board of Psychological Hypnosis. He is a Clinical Member and Approved Supervisor in the American Association for Marriage and Family Therapy, a Member of the Society for Personality Assessment, American Group Psychotherapy Association, International Rorschach Society, Virginia and North Carolina Psychological Associations, and the American Psychological Association. He has been in full-time practice as a clinical psychologist in public and private mental health clinics, in state mental hospitals, and in private practice since 1970. His original clinical research has been published regularly in professional journals and presented at state, regional, and national professional conferences. In 1982 Division 18 of the American Psychological Association presented Dr. MacHovec with a national Certificate of Recognition for his contributions to the field.

Figure 16 *(continued)*

FEES

```
Psychotherapy, hypnotherapy, testing....... $55 per
                                       50-minute hour
Group therapy................. $20 single, $35 couple
                                       90-minute sessions
Consultation........... charged at hourly rate plus any
                               required written report
                               or special preparation
```

PAYMENT

Payment is due when services are provided, in cash, by check, or MasterCard or Visa credit cards. Services stop if $100 or more in arrears or past due for more than 30 days. Please advise if payment of fees becomes a financial hardship. You will be charged for appointments not kept if not cancelled 24 hours in advance. Dr. MacHovec is an authorized Blue Cross Provider.

CONFIDENTIALITY

Psychological services are considered confidential and are protected by professional ethics and by law. No information obtained in therapy sessions will be given to anyone without your specific written consent except by a judge's direct or court order or when your life or others are in clear and imminent danger.

TAPING

Due to legal and ethical considerations, Dr. MacHovec reserves the right to tape record any therapy sessions. Only date and time are used to identify tapes (no names). Tapes are considered confidential and erased after two years.

OFFICE LOCATION

Professional office is at 145 Marshall Terrace, Danville, Virginia, south off Mount Vernon, north off Watson Street. Phone 804-797-2522 for further directions.

Figure 16 *(continued)*

P S Y C H O L O G I C A L   S E R V I C E S

INDIVIDUAL PSYCHOTHERAPY is 1-to-1 therapist-client treatment of specific personal problems.

GROUP THERAPY usually consists of 5-9 persons who meet together to share problems and help each other in processing them and to experiment with solutions.

MARRIAGE, DIVORCE, FAMILY, SEX THERAPIES are all specific applications of individual and group therapy methods to focus on special problem areas.

CLINICAL HYPNOSIS is a specialized form of psychotherapy which the American Psychiatric and the American Psychological Associations feel should be provided only by specially trained, licensed behavioral specialists.

PSYCHOLOGICAL ASSESSMENT (testing). Licensed Clinical Psychologists are the only behavioral specialists licensed to provide the full range of psychological tests (intelligence, personality, brain damage).

SPECIALTY GROUPS meet on a regular basis to meet special needs of the group (divorced, singles, teens, women, etc.). Such groups usually meet 90-minutes per session for ten sessions.

CONSULTATIVE SERVICES are special services to business, government, and the local community in areas relevant to psychology (communications, human relations, stress management, etc.).

———

Frank J. MacHovec PhD
Licensed Clinical Psychologist
145 Marshall Terrace
Danville, Virginia 24541

PHONE: 804-797-2522

Figure 16 *(continued)*

For Life is to be Enjoyed not endured!

J. Davis Mannino ~ Psychotherapist ~ 2101 Hayes Street, San Francisco, Ca. 94117 ~ (415)752-398

April, 1983

WHAT YOU SHOULD KNOW ABOUT OUR CLIENT-THERAPIST RELATIONSHIP

1. Payment is due at the completion of each session.

2. My professional fees are tax deductible as medical expenses. Save your cancelled checks. They are your receipt for services rendered.

3. Please note my professional fees are not reimbursible under all insurance policies. I am not responsible for policies which do not cover all or part of my professional fee. Insurance forms will be completed if submitted in a timely fashion. Check with your insurance carrier for procedures.

4. 24 hours is the minimum advance notice to cancel an appointment. Missed appointments will be billed at one half of session fee for the first missed appointment. Thereafter, the full fee is charged. Repeated missed appointments or lateness will result in discontinuation of the client-therapist relationship.

5. There is   strict client-therapist confidentiality. Total confidentiality is adhered to. No discussion of your case will occur without a signed release by you on file. In social settings I always refer to my clients as friends and you may do likewise. I never, ever refer to my clients in public as clients nor hint or discuss in any way, form or fashion their backgrounds or cases, or that they are even clients of mine.

6. The only exceptions to client-therapist confidentiality are: (1) should you tell others; (2) you have signed a release for me to provide information to an insurance company, physician or other such professional; (3) those rare instances when a client fails to pay an outstanding bill and a collection agency or other recovery means is utilized. Information given in these rare circumstances will be only the minimum information necessary to facilitate collection of professional fees owing.

7. It is the client's responsibility to bring a tape for recording to each session. They are the exclusive property of the client It is the client's responsbility to listen to each tape prior to the next session.

8. The client-therapist relationship may terminate without prejudice at the discretion of either the client or therapist.

-MORE-

Figure 17

Page Two
April, 1983

9. I subscribe to full disclosure principles. Resume' materials concerning my education, professional experience, training, writings and professional associations is available to anyone upon request.

10. Inquiries, complaints and/or concerns regarding my competence, fitness to practice psychotherapy and/or professional ethics should be directed to the California Department of Consumer Affairs' Board of Behavioral Science Examiners, 1021 "O" Street, Sacramento, California 95814. My license number   LX 007550 is "posted in public view at my place of practice," and expires October 31, 1984

11. I welcome referrals and will provide one free "exploratory session" to anyone you suggest compliments of both you and I.

12. I am always open to comments, compliments and criticisms. I welcome your trust in me and am prepared to work hard to assist you actualize your therapeutic goals and objectives.

Thank You.

Figure 17 (*continued*)

ALLAN G. HEDBERG, Ph.D. _____

CLINICAL PSYCHOLOGIST
LICENSE NUMBER PS 4xxx

SHAW-SIXTH SQUARE
5100 NORTH SIXTH STREET, SUITE 130
FRESNO, CALIFORNIA 93710

209 / 227-8471

BLAME

The aggressive attitude reacts to circumstances with blame.
We blame ourselves or someone else, or God, or if we can't find
a tangible scapegoat, we blame "fate." What an absolute waste!
When we blame ourselves, we multiply our guilt, we rivet ourselves to the past (another "dangling" unchangeable), and we
decrease our already low self-esteem. If we choose to blame
someone else or God, we cut off that source of power and help
in resolving the problem. Doubt replaces trust, and we put
down roots of bitterness that can make us cynical. If we blame
others, we enlarge the distance between us and them. We alienate.
We poison a relationship. We settle for something much less than
whatever could have been. And on top of all that, we do not find
relief!

          Blame never affirms, it assaults.
          Blame never restores, it wounds.
          Blame never solves, it complicates.
          Blame never unites, it separates.
          Blame never smiles, it frowns.
          Blame never forgives, it rejects.
          Blame never forgets, it remembers.
          Blame never builds, it destroys.

Let's admit it--not until we stop blaming will we start enjoying
health and happiness again! This was underscored as I read the
following words recently:

          . . . one of the most innovative psychologist in this
          half of the twentieth century . . . said recently that
          he considers only one kind of counselee relatively
          hopeless: that person who blames other people for his
          or her problems. If you can own the mess you're in, he
          says, there is hope for you and help available. As long
          as you blame others, you will be a victim for the rest
          of your life.

Blame backfires, hurting us more than the object of our resentment.

          Modified, but Taken From: Strenthening Your Grip
                                      By Charles Swindoll

JUST THINKING:

Few things help an individual more than to place responsibility
upon him and to let him know that you trust him.

                                      Booker T. Washington

Figure 18

ALLAN G. HEDBERG, Ph.D. _____

CLINICAL PSYCHOLOGIST
LICENSE NUMBER PS 4208

SHAW-SIXTH SQUARE
5100 NORTH SIXTH STREET, SUITE
FRESNO, CALIFORNIA 93710

209 / 227-8471

DO I MAKE A DIFFERENCE?

In some way, however small and secret, each of us is a little mad . . . Everyone is lonely at bottom and cries to be understood; but we can never entirely understand someone else, and each of us remains part stranger even to those who love us . . . It is the weak who are cruel--gentleness is to be expected only from the strong . . . Those who do not know fear are not really brave, for courage is the capacity to confront what can be imagined . . . You can understand people better if you look at them--no matter how old or impressive they may be--as if they are children. For most of us never mature; we simply grow taller . . . Happiness comes only when we push our brains and hearts to the farthest reaches of which we are capable.

. . . The purpose of life is to matter--to count to stand for something, to have it make some difference that we lived at all.

(Author Unknown)

A CREDO: MY RELATIONSHIP WITH YOU

You and I are in a relationship which I value and want to keep. Yet each of us is a separate person with his own unique needs and the right to try to meet those needs. I will try to be genuinely accepting of your behavior both when you are trying to meet your needs and when you are having problems meeting your needs.

When you share your problems, I will try to listen acceptingly and understandingly in a way that will facilitate your finding your own solutions rather than depending upon mine. When you have a problem because my behavior is interfering with your meeting your needs, I encourage you to tell me openly and honestly how you are feeling. At those times, I will listen and then try to modify my behavior.

However, when your behavior interferes with my meeting my own needs, thus causing me to feel unaccepting of you, I will tell you as openly and honestly as I can exactly how I am feeling, trusting that you respect my needs enough to listen and then try to modify your behavior.

At those times when either of us cannot modify his behavior to meet the needs of the other, thus finding that we have a conflict-of-needs in our relationship, let us commit ourselves to resolve each such conflict without ever resorting to the use of either my power or yours to win at the expense of the other losing. I respect your needs, but I also must respect my own. Consequently, let us strive always to search for solutions to our inevitable conflicts that will be acceptable to both of us. In this way, your needs will be met, but so will mine--no one will lose, both will win.

As a result, you can continue to develop as a person through meeting your needs, but so can I. Our relationship can always be a healthy one because it will be mutually satis- fying . Thus, each of us can become what he is capable of being, and we can continue to relate to each other in mutual respect, friendship, love and peace.

Figure 19

Vol. 3 No. 2

"YOU KNOW WHAT I MEAN...?"

Learn to Communicate Clearly

from the desk of...

DR. SUSAN STURDIVANT

If I had to choose one thing that is the key to successful people relationships, it would be Communication Skills. Communication is the lifeline of both business and personal relationships, and is the essence of psychotherapy.

Many problems that arise between people can be traced to a breakdown in communications. When something seems crystal clear to us, it's hard to remember that it may not be so obvious to others; to realize that our business associates, spouses, children and friends may need clarification or explanation in order to understand our point of view.

At other times, our words and our actions may send mixed messages, creating confusion instead of clear communication. If I say, "I'm glad to see you" with a frown on my face, am I happy or not? The signals are conflicting.

Like the tango, successful communication takes two. Since we move back and forth from speaker to listener many times in a conversation, this issue of the *UPDATE on Human Behavior* contains information to help improve both your speaking and listening skills.

Most of us assume that if we can speak and hear, we can communicate. In fact, it's not nearly that simple. What we say *verbally* constitutes only 3% of all that we communicate. The other 97% is made up of how we look and sound and feel, plus all the interpretations we make of what others say, — as well as the setting in which it all occurs!

Along with the actual words we speak, we communicate through gestures, body language, tone of voice, and facial expressions. The timing of what we say is as important as the words we use. What we *don't* say often has as much impact as what we *do* say.

So we see that if I speak and you listen, I may be transmitting information, but that's all. But if I speak, and you listen, and *we* understand, then we are communicating.

The Communication Process

Communication is not just an event, but a *process* - a process that requires the cooperation and understanding of both parties.

The communication process has three distinct components

- what you MEAN to say: the message you intend to send
- HOW you say it: nonverbal cues such as tone of voice, facial expression, & body posture that accompany the spoken words.
- how the listener INTERPRETS what you have said.

Successful communication occurs when all parts of the message are clearly spoken, accompanied by congruent nonverbal signals. When there is a difference between the spoken word and the nonverbal signals, the nonverbal will be dominant. A 'No...?" delivered hesitant-

ly and in a soft tone of voice, for instance, is heard as a "maybe". "No." stated firmly with direct eye contact is more likely to be believed as a definite refusal, while "No!" means "Absolutely not... and don't ask again!"

Where We Go Awry

Too often, we make the mistake of assuming that others will understand more than we actually say to them. In personal relationships, for example, we may expect our intimates to be able to "read our minds" because they know us so well. "She ought to know how I feel" you may say to yourself, even though you have said nothing about your feelings. Business associates who work together closely also fall into this trap, thinking: "He knows how important this project is, so he understands that I need his data as soon as possible."

In other situations, communication is misinterpreted because our words reflect our emotional state more than our intended message. For example a pressured manager asks his assistant for sales data necessary for an important presentation the next day. He *means* to convey that the project is absolutely top priority. But he frames the message, "Don't leave today until those figures are on my desk." His assistant responding to the impatience with which the message is delivered *interprets*: "Why is he mad at me?"

On other occasions, the distortion may come from the emotional state of the listener: A wife tells her children not to bother their father. She means to tell her husband, "I'm protecting you from being disturbed." Her husband, sensitive to his children's shyness around him, overhears and interprets, "There she goes again, making me a bad guy to the kids."

5307 East Mockingbird, Suite 401   Dallas, Texas 75206   (214) 821-3467

Figure 20

Figure 21

Advertising

Therapists who advertise have concentrated their efforts on newspapers. These are a good value because their comparatively low cost allows you to run them repeatedly, giving you more exposure and increasing the chances you'll be remembered. When it comes to promoting services choose local over regional publications. Some marketing experts advise that you're better off splitting ads between local papers rather than paying the premium for having your ad in a high circulation paper. Moreover, you can test different ads for different effects so you'll have data on which kind of ads get responses from various target segments. Splitting ads between newspapers can also give you the opportunity to test various elements contained in your ad, such as size or whether fee is mentioned.

We've selected some examples of both display and classified ads that have been used successfully by therapists. These ads represent many of the points about copywriting we made above. For instance, Grover Loughmiller, Ph.D. ran an ad that emulates a news story, while Richard Tractman, Ph.D. of Port Jefferson Station, NY used an ad that contained long copy with a headline designed to appeal to reader self-interest.

Find Suitable Career Goals
At The Loughmiller Institute

Loughmiller Institute located at 422 S. Spring in Tyler can help you decide what line of work or career for which you are best qualified by administering career and vocational tests by computer or on an individual basis.

Ten years after graduation from college, 75 percent of graduates are in a profession other than the one for which they were trained.

Recent studies estimate that 25 percent of all U.S. workers (24 million) are unhappy in their jobs.

Too many people think that finding an occupation or a college major is a fairly insignificant decision and do not stop to think that they'll be spending half of their waking hours for the rest of their lives doing a designated activity.

The research has found that occupations tend to fall into six major categories or groupings. They include realistic, investigative, artistic, social service, enterprising ad conventional. With a fairly high degree of accuracy, testing ca n determine for which of the six categories a person would be best suited and to a somewhat lesser degree of accuracy, the specific occupations within that group for which they would be best fitted.

When you think of the amount of money that goes into the average persons education, apprenticeship, or on-the-job training, and then think of what it would colst to change occupations 10 years later,

the cost of testing becomes insignificant. This doesn't include the unhappiness, the lost wages, the mental stress, etc.

Many people think vocational testing is merely testing for vocational interests like many people had in high school. A full vocational battery of tests is much more comprehensive than that. A test of abilities, and tests of personality variables related to work dimensions (e.g.,ability to get along with people smoothly, etc.) are also given. The reason that all these types of areas need to be sampled is that a person may have an interest in an occupation for which they are not suited by ability, or they have may both the ability and interest for an occupation but may not be suited temperamentally for the occupation.

Many people in East Texas have assumed that it is necessary to go to large metropolitan areas such as Dallas or Shreveport to obtain good career/vocational testing and counseling. This is not true.

Testing at the Loughmiller Institute can be done either by computer or by tests personally administered by the psychologist (or by some combination of the two). Many of the tests for vocational interest and perosnality can be done by computer less expensively and with greater accuracy and thoroughness than can be done by individually administered

tests. The computer is not magical but simply is able to take the best thinking of a lot of psychologists and incorporate it in a program.

The amount of testing and the cost of testing is dictated by the thoroughness with which the person wishes to explore vocational areas. You receive a full 20-page typewritten report which is included in the cost of the test.

From this written report and consultation individuals can obtain a quite accurate notion of what general area(s) for which they are best suited with a listing of 50 to 150 specific occupations that would be most suitable. Research has shown a high proportion of people who go into areas for which comprehensive testing shows them to be fitted end up ten years later happy in those occupations.

Testing is appropriate for anyone 13 to 14 years of age and older. It is particularly appropriate for people exiting high school and for perosns who may be dissatisfied in their current occupation but are not sure which alternative directions to take. It is also appropriate for women who may have been out ot the work force for some time and may be reentering the job market.

Call the Loughmiller Institute and let them help you choose the career which is right for you. Longview 214/753-7496 or Tyler 214/593-8395.

Figure 22

SELF IMAGE: KEY TO SUCCESS IN ALL AREAS OF LIFE

By. Dr. Richard Trachtman

Most people have some ideas of their self image, what they think of themselves, but very few realize how crucial attitudes about one's self are to achieving a happy and fulfilling life. A poor self image can lead to repeated disappointments and frustrations in love, work, friendship and family life as well as in activities such as finding a place to live, calling a repairman or trying to diet. To make matters worse, everyone's self image is partly unconscious, and unconscious attitudes about one's self can affect a person's behavior in negative ways that he or she can not control.

After 20 years working as a psychotherapist, I am very familiar with how people sabotage themselves without knowing what they are doing. One of my patients was an attractive and intelligent woman, who was secretly convinced that no worthwhile man could love her. Unerringly she fell for self centered users who exploited her sexually but showed little real interest in her needs. In the meantime she ignored other, more appropriate men who seemed genuinely interested in her. Without knowing it she was obeying her unconscious mind, which told her she could not have a man who would treat her well.

How can you tell if you have problems with self image? If you find yourself behaving like the people described above, you have a problem. Some other signs of poor self image are the following: always feeling that other people are smarter, better looking, luckier or more deserving; being hesitant to ask for a raise when others are paid more, to ask someone for a date, to raise your hand in class or to ask a question; letting someone sell you something you don't really want; always letting others have their way; not telling someone that they have hurt your feelings or annoyed you because you are afraid they will get angry or ignore you. If any of these signs are typical of you it is likely that poor self image stands between you and a more happy and fulfilling life. But, don't despair, self image can be improved with the help of psychotherapy.

Psychotherapy for problems of self image and for other problems is available by appointment at the office of **Richard Trachtman, Ph.D., 108 Terryville Road, Box 154, Port Jefferson Station, N.Y. 11776. Phone: (516) 928-1454.**

Figure 23

THOSE WHO FORGET THE PAST ARE DOOMED TO RELIVE IT.
Best Wishes for Gay Pride Week, Summer and always

- Ten years of committed, creative professional experience
- Senior University Instructor, Human Relations
- Five fresh, positive years in private practice
- Credentialed and licensed Psychotherapist #L7550
- GGBA Member

For Life is to be Enjoyed, not Endured!
J. DAVIS MANNINO, PSYCHOTHERAPIST
415/752-3983 By Appointment

Figure 24

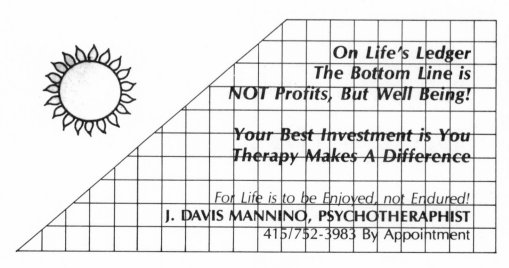

*On Life's Ledger
The Bottom Line is
NOT Profits, But Well Being!*

*Your Best Investment is You
Therapy Makes A Difference*

For Life is to be Enjoyed, not Endured!
J. DAVIS MANNINO, PSYCHOTHERAPHIST
415/752-3983 By Appointment

Figure 25

PSYCHOLOGICAL SERVICES INCORPORATED❖

Medical Arts Building, Suite 200
1438 Defense Highway (Rt. 450E)
Crofton, Maryland 21114

- Counseling: Adults - Adolescents - Children - Single Parents
- Therapy: Family - Marital   Sexual
- Training: Relationship - Communications - Parenting Skills
- Consultation: School and Behavioral Problems
- Divorce Mediation and Counseling
- Treatment: Chemical Dependencies - Adults and Adolescents
- Stress Management ● Hypnosis ● Biofeedback
- Testing: Psychological, Educational and Vocational
- Consultation: Industries, Agencies, Schools, and Attorneys
- Health Insurance-Qualified Services Available
     from Multi-Disciplinary Staff

For Appointments call **261-1449**

❖Accredited by International Association of Counseling Services, Incorporated

Figure 26

SINGLE PARENTS
*Does Your Child Have Any
Of These 10 Problems?*
☐ Angry outbursts
☐ Excessive crying or sadness
☐ Drop in grades since the
   separation
☐ Fighting at school
☐ Teachers reporting
   daydreaming
☐ Loss of interest in friends or
   usual pastimes
☐ Babyish behavor
☐ Being "too good"
☐ Playing one parent against the
   other

If the answer is yes, your youngster may
profit from individual or group treatment
for the special problems of children of
separated/divorced parents.

Rachelle Dorfman, M.S.S.
Psychotherapist
Hours by appointment
No Charge for initial consultation
355-7143

Figure 27

ALLERGIES
they are often aggravated by stress, anxiety and tension. Learn to manage these allergy related emotions.
for information or appointment call Stephen Pew Ph.D.
ADAPTIVE BEHAVIOR CLINIC
330-0955

DO DIETS WORK?
There are healthier and more permanent solutions.
for information or appointment call Stephen Pew Ph.D.
ADAPTIVE BEHAVIOR CLINIC
330-0955

MIGRAINES
are often caused by unmanaged stress. Learn self-hypnosis to manage your health.
for information or appointment call Stephen Pew Ph.D.
ADAPTIVE BEHAVIOR CLINIC
330-0955

SELF HYPNOSIS WORKS
Learn to manage your own
- Migraines
- Stress
- Weight
- Health

for information or appointment call Stephen Pew Ph.D.
ADAPTIVE BEHAVIOR CLINIC
330-0955

Figure 28

Are you looking for a responsible therapist but feeling overwhelmed by the multitude of choices?

Recognizing the importance of a correct matching, I offer a free consultation to determine mutual suitability. Individual, Couple Counseling and Psychotherapy.

Keith Breiman C.S.W.
580-2800

N.Y.S. Certified
Insurance Accepted

Figure 29

Why Weight?

Join a FAT CLASS now!

Feel GOOD . . . Look BETTER

Be your BEST!

Call Meramec Counseling

727-0613

Marian Hirsch, MSW   Linda Pilcher, MSW

CLASSES FORMING NOW FOR FALL

Figure 30

STRESS, SADNESS, or Silence in your home? There is help! Vicki Burnett Marriage and Family Therapist, 236-6452. Day and Evening appointments.

Figure 31

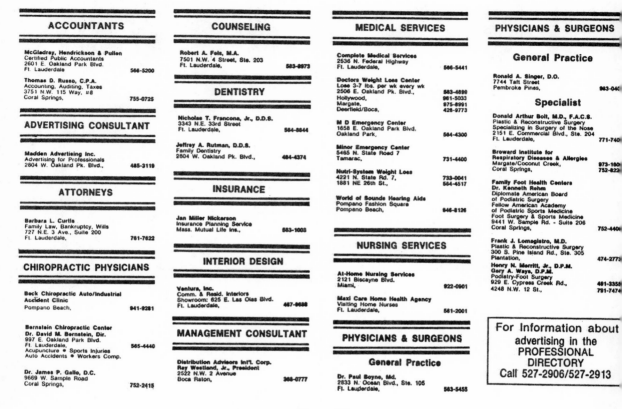

Figure 32

Following TV and newspapers in popularity is direct mail advertising. If you want to use this method it's probably a good policy to check any ideas you have for direct mailings with a couple of colleagues before you begin. Although it's acceptable to use mailouts for establishing contacts with referral agents and communicating with current clients you may run into an ethical dilemma by attempting to solicit clients directly.

Other media for advertising include posters, billboards, signs, car cards (i.e., on buses and subway cars) handbills, and skywriting. Specialty items like pens, matchbooks, coffee mugs, ashtrays, rulers and the like with slogans, logos, or brief messages have been used by many merchants and manufacturers but have been virtually ignored by the therapist. One therapist who has used an alternative promotional medium is J. Davis Mannino, of San Francisco. He came up with a handbill that incorporates his slogan "For life is to be enjoyed, not endured."

Had Your Fall Service?

- ☑ Brakes
- ☑ Transmission
- ☑ Oil
- ☑ Lube
- ☑ Filter

- ☐ Relationship (or lack of it) problems
- ☑ Job Satisfaction
- ☐ Purpose and Direction
- ☐ Alcohol or Drug Problems
- ☑ General Contentment

People are funny animals. We operate with such a high regard for our possessions and yet all too often with such little regard for own needs. Our lives also need regular maintenance and occasional fine tuning. Taking stock every so often clears the air. After all, shouldn't our most important priority be *ourselves?*

Credentials, experience and concern add up to a great track record. Call for an appointment. "For life is to be enjoyed, not endured."

J. Davis Mannino   752-3983

LICENSED PSYCHOTHERAPIST L.C.S.W. #7550

Figure 33

Publicity

It's generally not too difficult to get publicity for yourself or your practice. One of the easiest ways is to prepare a news release and send it in to local media. Most newspapers have a section devoted to local business people who've gotten promoted or got elected to offices within their professional or fraternal organization. If you publish an article in a journal, get board certified, win an award, develop some innovative treatment procedure, or just attend a national convention you can submit a news release about yourself and your practice.

For some reason the folks down at the local newspapers and radio stations are kind of fussy about the form they are willing to consider for receiving information. To avoid the prospect of your submission not being used because you failed to abide by the rules, we'll show you how to prepare a news release.

Begin with 8½ x 11 white paper, preferably with your letterhead. It's important that a contact person be identified along with a phone number where s/he can be reached for more information in case any is wanted (sometimes news releases lead to inteviews). It's customary to indicate this person by stating "contact" followed by the name. Then you indicate that the information contained below is "For Immediate Release" by typing these words, followed by the date. Do not use the words "news" or "important." Let the editors decide if it's newsworthy. Then write a headline. Type the copy with double spacing throughout. If you get to the bottom of the page and have more copy, type the word "-MORE-" on a line by itself and go on. Do not break paragraphs by having them on more than one page. If it appears you cannot finish it, stop at the end of the previous paragraph, type "-MORE-" under it and start on the next page. If you've used more than one page type either "-END-" or "###" when you have said all you intend to.

As you can see, preparing a news release is rather simple. What's important to do is make sure that you give the editors sufficient lead time to get your item on the calendar. It's recommended that it be in the editor's hand a week to 10 days before you expect publication or broadcast. A sample of a release has been provided by Miriam Easton Berger, M.S.W. and is reprinted here.

relationship counseling
holistic health counseling
group therapy
brief therapy
home visits
in person/by phone

Miriam Easton Berger, M.S.W
psychotherapist
L.C.S.W. #8934

Option Center for Psychotherapy

Self-Healing Center
963 Grand Avenue
Pacific Beach, CA 92109
(714) 270-4900

Miriam Easton Berger, LCSW
270-4900 or
home: 272-3379

"Would you like to be still happier than you are?"
This is a question with which Miriam Easton Berger, LCSW, begins
a seminar in Option Process, which helps, not only people with
definable emotional problems, but also the ordinary person to
feel better in daily life. Option Therapy uses a Socratic
method of questioning, which assists us to sift through layers
of counter-productive beliefs that interfere with inner peace
and comfortable relationships. For example, "What are you
afraid would happen if you didn't use the psychological whip on
yourself?" A typical response is, "If I accepted myself, as I
am, I'm afraid I'd never change. I berate myself when I do not
live up to my standards, in order to discipline myself." The
next question is, "Is there a positive way you could motivate
yourself to grow and change, such as, accentuating the wanting
to make that particular change?"

Most psychotherapies originated on the West Coast, and were
brought East. Option Process originated in the East, and has
recently been brought to San Diego by Miriam Easton Berger, MSW,
Director of the Option Center for Psychotherapy.

Ms Berger will be giving a free introductory lecture,
including self-help skills, on Tuesday, April 20, 7:30 P.M.
at the Self-Healing Center (see green flier enclosed). For
further information, she can be reached at 270-4900 or at home:
272-3379.

Figure 34

Another kind of promotion that you can use is a news article written
by you that is submitted to a newspaper. Small newspapers are often un-
derstaffed. Their editors frequently are forced to use items from wire
services. If these are weekly papers their objective is to carry articles that
are relevant to local readers. So, you may find that your submission
may be welcomed with open arms and published with your by-line,
which means they put your name under the title. We've included a couple of examples here of therapist authored newspaper articles.

FLORIDA'S LARGEST WEEKLY NEWSPAPER   **OUR 22nd YEAR**

Serving Hallandale, Hollywood, Aventura, North Miami Beach & North Dade   Member of Florida Press Assn. and National Newspaper Assn.

HALLANDALE DIGEST

Vol. 22 No. 4   Established 1963   43,000 AUDITED CIRCULATION   48 Pages in 6 Sections   September 6, 1984

How to get what you want

By Dr. Alan Schlaks Ph.D.

Many people are shy and watch life pass them by. They will usually leave a situation angry because they do not express what they would have liked to express. Some choose to be this way for fear of being rejected, "needing" approval from significant others, or fear of making the other person angry. If you find you are non-assertive, self-denying, inhibited, and emotionally dishonest here are some ways to learn to be assertive and get what you want in life.

Definition of Assertion: An open, honest, direct and appropriate communication of your thoughts, wishes, opinions or feeling which

1. does not violate your rights
2. does not violate the rights of another person by attempting to demean, belittle, humiliate or in any way "put them down" as a person, and which
3. eventually does not cause you undue anxiety or guilt

Personal Rights:

The right to be treated with respect.

The right to have feeling and express them, including complaints and criticisms.

The right to be listened to and taken seriously; to receive emotional response, clarification, support.

The right to set one's own priorities.

The right to say no without feeling guilty.

Assertive Behavior:

1. When expressing refusal, express a decisive, "no," explain why you are refusing, but don't be unduly apologetic. When applicable, offer the other person an alternative suggestion or course of action.

2. Give as prompt and brief a reply as you can, without interruptions.

3. Insist on being treated with fairness and justice.

4. Request an explanation when asked to do something unreasonable.

5. Look the other person in the eye. Check your other body language for things that might convey indirectness or lack of self-assurance (e.g., hand over mouth, shuffling feet). Watch your voice tone and inflection, making sure your voice is neither a sub-audible whisper nor overly-loud.

6. When expressing annoyance or criticism, remember: Comment on the person's **behavior**, rather than attack him or her.

7. When commenting on another's behavior, try to use "I Statements". Ex.: "When you keep cancelling out on social arrangements at the last minute, it causes a lot of inconvenience to me and I feel really annoyed." Where possible, offer a suggestion for an alternative behavior: "I think we'd better sit down and try to figure out a better way of planning our time together so we can cut down on this kind of inconveniencing."

8. Be clear about your **goals** in asserting yourself. Do I want to placate the other person, or to prove to her/him that I'm better and smarter than she/he? Or do I want to express some of my upset feelings and also let her/him know I care very much for her/him? Try to tease out self-defeating or hidden agendas and replace them with more communication-facilitating goals.

9. In thinking about the situation, try to replace your anger, anxiety, and guilt-eliciting thoughts with more adaptive, calm-producing ones.

We will be answering questions about the personal problems you may want feedback on.

Please mail your questions to: Dr. Alan Schlaks, 4700-E Sheridan St., Hollywood, Fla. 33021

Figure 35

The "Outside" Father

by Dr. Emanuel Plesent

As was indicated in a recent issue of SPOTLIGHT ON SINGLES, in more than 90% of separation - divorces, the mother retains custody of any children. The father leaves the house and usually maintains some degree of contact through visitation, telephone or letters. Being out of the house, he becomes the "outsider looking in." While viewed by some as having it made...after all, he pops in and out getting the best, and not having to handle the often very difficult day to day efforts necessary for individuals and the family to survive...he nevertheless has a variety of concerns with which to deal. This article will explore some of these concerns and propose a guideline to deal with a major complicating factor, that of guilt. While these concerns certainly vary with each situation, some that often appear include, adapting to a new environment, changing roles and relationships with ex-spouse and

helpful. Often however, involvement of friends or family may be counterproductive. Objective professional guidance may be of great assistance at this crucial period.

Recently, support groups for men have made gains. Traditionally, women have found it easier to express their concerns to others, reach out for help, and accept emotional support. Men, traditionally, have found it more difficult to express their unhappiness to others and accept emotional support. This is gradually changing. In some ways, this is an outgrowth of the women's movement. As women were freed from certain traditional roles and views, concurrently men have also been freed.

While initial and subsequent phases may overlap and may occur very rapidly, for the sake of clarity, I have separated them.

After the initial rearrangement phase and new roles and relationships start to take shape, additional situations may

visiting father. This in itself can be a very traumatic period of time for all concerned.

As children become teenagers and then become young adults, points of contact change. Visitation may be arranged directly with the children, now adults, perhaps in their own households. They build their own lives in which the visiting father may have less and less involvement. On the other hand, the relationship may become even better than before if they will permit a revised mature relationship. How people deal with the changing situations is the key to happiness. All too often people utilize guilt and unhappiness for whatever purposes people use guilt and unhappiness.

As touched upon before, guilt is an emotion often encountered not only in father-children relationships, but also in many aspects of life. The overwhelming majority of people would say that guilt is an unhappy, negative feeling. Many of us try to "do something" to ease the bad

"Upon leaving the house, the father may have feelings of having failed his father role, abandoned the children"

children, and questions about the future. Of course, these same concerns apply to the mother, as well. I'd like to focus on father-children relationship and some of the thoughts and emotions that may occur.

Upon leaving the house, the father may have feelings of having failed his father role, abandoned the children, and/or confusion as to how to maintain a relationship with the children. In some instances, merely visiting the children may bring up distressed emotions. Unresolved bitterness between the parents may erupt at this time. The father might reduce or abandon his visitations altogether. On the other hand, the father might visit and/or, telephone several time a week attempting to keep a similar or in fact, a more involved role with the children than prior to the separation or divorce. During this initial, most trying, transitional time, support from friends or extended family may be

occur. In time, the new arrangements may settle into a new routine. A "honeymoon" stage may occur with everyone, parents and children fulfilling the new responsibilities. The visiting father may faithfully see the children. The mother may make sure there are no interfering circumstances and the children may be cooperative and look forward to the visits. Of course, some or all of the above may not occur if the situation is confused and the working through of the many issues is blocked. Certainly the age of the children is a major factor. Are the children babies or grown-up and on their own? There are many variations of the theme.

For some visiting fathers; there may be overriding guilt feelings. They may be afraid to say "no" to the children, may be accused of "spoiling" the children, etc. The father and the children may have problems with the "Disciplinary" roles. Any or all of them may want so much or so little from their time together. The visiting parent may feel like a parent and at the same time not feel like a parent. The limited time may encroach on the perceived parental role. On the other hand, in many instances, the relationship may improve and may be more productive than before the separation or divorce.

With the passing of more time, and as children become older, it is possible for the urgency or lonversely the avoidance of contact to be modified. The pendulum may swing back and forth. Frequent visits may become less frequent, or less frequent visits might become more frequent. Children may express their anger or their wish for the parents to get back together, or pit one parent against the other. As new relationships come into the lives of the parents, the children may respond with acceptance, confusion, testing, relief, etc. The same may occur in either or both of the parents. For children, the adjustment to new, significant adults in their lives poses additional tasks to work through.

As each of the parents rebuilds hi/her own personal life, additional situations come up for the visiting father. For example, remarriage of the ex-wife presents the complication of who is Dad and who is Father? Of course, the terms are only used to indicate the possible confusion that needs to be sorted out by the visiting father, the children, as well as the mother and new husband. A similar series of concerns are involved if the visiting father remarries.

Another situation that may come up, especially with teenagers is the desire of the child to live permanently with the

feelings surrounding guilt. Many of us feel guilty and do nothing more than feel badly about feeling guilty. A question to ask ourselves is, "What is the purpose of feeling guilty?" A second question would be, "What would we be afraid might happen if we didn't feel guilty?" If we could then ask ourselves to find ways to react in a productive and constructive manner without feeling guilty then we could break through the negative binds within which we place ourselves. While guilt feelings may motivate some visiting fathers to do positive things, the same feelings drastically reduce the freedom of positive choice in relation to the children. In turn, the children may feel guilty about the father feeling guilty and so on, and so on, and so on. Therefore, this author most strongly advocates that fathers (and all of us) work to free themselves from guilt as a motivation and replace it with the positive desire to be the best we can be under a most difficult situation.

One man who has been a visiting father for more than fifteen years recently had a most revealing experience. His son, age 20, was telling him how bad a father he had been to abandon him 15 years before. Why hadn't he been a better father, etc.? The son had voiced this theme many times through the years, but this time the father responded differently. He said, "I'm sorry if you were hurt, but I just don't feel guilty anymore. I did the best I could. I could do no more." To the father's surprise, the son then put his arm around his father and said, "You're some guy, Dad. Thanks!"... And then they both were free.

This article has touched upon a few of the possible pressures carried by the visiting father and suggested an approach which may lead to a more positive, constructive way of relating to his children. This author holds that using this approach will be healthier for the father, the children, the mother and the situation. The author remains very aware of the usually extreme pressures on the parent who has the primary custodial role. It is also hoped that a greater awareness on the part of the mother of the concerns and pressures of the father will lead to a less stressful relationship, this would relieve a major source of stress on the mother, as well.

NOTE: Dr. Emanuel Plesent, co-director of the Option Center for Psychotherapy, 79 Hillside Ave., Williston Park, N.Y. (516) 747-5335, is a psychotherapist who works with individuals, families and groups. Questions or comments pertaining to his article will be welcomed.

Figure 36

There are also a few tips that may help you in preparing news articles. Begin with a headline that gets people's attention. Sometimes it is referred to as a "grabber" for obvious reasons. In your first paragraph, known as the "lead," give a thumbnail summary of **who, what, where, when, how,** and **why.** The remaining paragraphs expand on the details of what you put in your lead. This is called the "body." Bear in mind that newswriting epitomizes concrete and simple wording. Also, if you want to use illustrative materials it's customary to include 8x10 glossy photographs in black and white. You can also get away with 5x7 prints but some printers don't like them. It's also helpful to date your photo and include a caption. Regardless of the size photos you end up using, don't expect to have them returned to you even if your submission is not published.

Large newspapers have several editors. Never send your news release to the managing editor. Instead, send it to the city editor or a section editor like "women's," "lifestyle," "family," and so on depending on the term used by the paper. Small newspapers may have only one editor for everything. If that's the case send your submission to her/him. Individual reporters work on assignment by editor so a submission to a reporter runs a higher risk of getting discarded.

Public Service Announcements (PSAs) are frequently used by nonprofit organizations. If you are interested you can prepare them as well. Perhaps the easiest to develop are PSAs for radio because they can be submitted in writing or you can go to the studio and record them. Each station has its own convention for length, so be sure to check before submitting a PSA. Here are a few examples of radio PSAs:

> Really listening to members of your family can improve relationships. An important first step is to make sure you understand the message. One way to do this is to restate what you think you heard without attacking it. This helps in seeing eye to eye. I'm Dr. _____ at the ABC Clinic.

Figure 37

Intimacy doesn't happen by itself in relationships. You have to work at it. Each partner must feel safe enough to share his or her personal feelings. Listen carefully to your partner and check for accuracy. This is Dr. _____ with an idea for living brought to you courtesy of (this station).

Figure 38

Many parents try to buy their children's love with material gifts. What children really want is your time spent willingly and enjoyably with them. Toys and clothes eventually wear out, but precious memories built during the growing years last a lifetime. I'm Dr. _____ on (station name) bringing you a message for better mental health.

Figure 39

If you're really energetic and highly motivated you may be able to write your own column. Some therapists have been able to do this. Some write columns on a regular basis. Others have made contributions only periodically which is understandable because writing a column requires a great deal of work. So, if you think this might be for you, make sure you are very committed to following through. Outlets for your articles are church, PTA, and organizational newsletters besides local newspapers. Allen Johnson, who you may recall hosts a weekly TV talk show also writes a weekly column for his city newspaper. One of Dr. Johnson's columns is reproduced here.

Family Focus —— *Fight fair in 1984*

If you make a New Year's resolution, I would suggest you consider this: If things are bugging you, relax and talk it over. This is easier said than done.

Do dad or the kids snack in front of the television set then leave all the dishes piled up there, or in the sink, for mom to face in the morning?

Do the kids throw their clothes on the floor and leave it to mom to pick them up? Or does mom squeeze the toothpaste from the top of the tube instead working her way up from the bottom?

Do these things upset you, but do you keep your feelings to yourself because they are too petty to fight over? Or perhaps you yell about it, but nothing seems to help.

If these things are happening to you, you're making a mistake. If you let things build up, you're sure to have one large-sized argument in the future.

Discussion, not yelling and screaming, in the New Year is crucial if the family is to grow well. There are usually stages that lead up to an argument. In the first stage, the person, who is upset keeps quiet even though they are bothered. Annoyances are brushed under the rug and not brought up for discussion—like the toothpaste tube—because the person thinks the problem is too petty.

Then you begin to think that if your spouse or child loved you, they would know what was bothering you. He or she would be able to read your mind. By this stage, you expect change without discussion.

Finally, you hit the argumentative stage. The petty things have built up and the result is a full-blown argument without any real discussion.

Arguments are not the way to solve a problem. Discussion is, because it leads to growth, understanding and the resolution of problems. Arguments impede growth. If you want growth, understanding, and resolution of problems, you need a real discussion.

Fair discussion does not put people down the way arguing usually does. When two people argue, often they don't hear each other because they perceive the comments as put-downs. Therefore, they don't listen. Teen-agers especially let things go right over their heads during an argument.

Fair discussion also means not bringing up treasures from the "treasure chest." These are incidents and bad experiences from the past that get dragged up when there is an argument. Once you bring up these treasures, you begin arguing about the past instead of the issue at hand.

Fair discussion means hearing what is said by the other person so you can repeat accurately what has been said. It shows the speaker that you have heard and understand what is being said. If you can truly listen and realize how you have hurt or been hurt, that leads to understanding and resolution of the problem.

Agreeing to disagree is a vital part of fair discussion. If two people have two different points of view, then you may need to agree to disagree with each other if a compromise is not possible. If, however, you don't agree to disagree, then you'll just yell and scream until you have the final say or more likely, get a sore throat.

Agreeing to disagree allows each person time to think about the other person's position. It leaves both with enough dignity (since there was no winner or loser) that they can come back in an hour and say, 'Maybe we weren't really so far apart after all.'

What's to be gained by fair discussion? It does not lead to a crisis situation. Arguments do lead to crisis. They are not calm and they put no one in the mood for discussion.

Discussions are based on mutual respect. Arguments are based on power struggles between people.

Arguing is based on an attempt for power. "The louder I yell, the more power I get" many people think is a truism. People must accept the fact that they can gain respect not by yelling louder than another person but by discussion.

Arguments are based on one-ups-manship. This is one of the problems with parent-teen relationships. Parents believe they are superior and yell to get that power across. But telling a teen that "I'm your parent, so I'm right" is not going to bring about the understanding that is desired.

There are a number of ground rules for fair fighting in the New Year.

•Don't let anything be swept under the rug, especially issues relating to money and sex. Those are the two issues people argue about the most.

•Don't believe that someone can read your thoughts, so you don't have to discuss problems.

•Strive for open communication this year. Say it and hear it. Realize that your spouse and children have a right to say what he or she feels. Accept the feelings of another even if they are different from yours.

•Think before speaking. Though this is hard for all of us, it makes communication much more clear.

•Put disagreements into a more positive context. Instead of saying "Don't spend anymore money," talk over family needs and discuss how everyone needs to save for family's goals.

•Try not to think that people who fight are letting it "all hang out" and that fighting's good for the soul. Words can come back to haunt you.

•Arguing sets a bad example for the kids. In future years, they will believe that the way to solve a problem is to fight. If you need to blow off steam—and everyone needs to—do it on the racquetball court.

•If a discussion grows into a argument, walk away. But remember to get back to a fair discussion—as discussed above—when each of you calm down.

This column is written by Dr. Allen F. Johnson, a child and family therapist. Dr. Johnson welcomes feedback sent to him at The Auburn Family Institute, 6 South Terrace.

Figure 40

Another way of getting publicity is to be interviewed by a reporter who's doing a story and contacts you as an expert. If you are known and have a high profile reporters will seek you out. The trick here is to be known and sought out. We know of no simple way to do this. However, if you offer to be on a few radio talk shows over a period of time you will get known around the station. When a need for a mental health expert arises the staff doing the piece usually asks around the station and your name is likely to come up and you may get a call. One marketing consultant told us that when he handled accounts he simply telephoned an editor at a newspaper where his client regularly bought advertising space and requested that a story be done on his client. He did not usually mention that the client was a purchaser of advertising space but he did offer an angle for an interesting story. Many cities have speakers' bureaus where you can register and indicate a special area of expertise. You may be contacted by a media representative by virtue of your listing or you may be contacted as a result of a speech you've made.

Here are some examples therapists have provided us of articles that have been written about them.

Exercise option to be happy

By Jean Bricarello
of The Daily Californian

Do you make yourself unhappy? Do you think it's natural to be unhappy?

And when you're unhappy, do you find yourself getting physically sick, maybe with a cold, a sore throat or stomach problems?

New York psychotherapist Miriam Easton Berger, temporarily making her home in El Cajon, would answer those questions — yes, no and probably yes.

The first two questions are key to what is called "Options Therapy," which, simplified, could be explained as exercising the option to be happy, or at least feel OK.

Berger who is an Options therapist, said the process is described fully in the book, "To Love is to be Happy With" By Barry Neil Kaufman.

"Most therapies," she said, "accept that it is natural to feel unhappy and frustrated under certain circumstances. Option Process challenges the belief that it is natural to feel unhappy. We believe that happiness, or at least feeling OK, is the normal state most of us would be in most of the time if we weren't making ourselves unhappy."

The Options idea is one of the subjects Berger is teaching while in El Cajon for the winter. "Options for Achieving Greater Happiness" is offered through the University of California at San Diego Extension, as is her class, "Self-Healing: Harnessing the Placebo Effect."

In a way, the two subjects are related. Options therapy is a form of self-healing, too.

"The idea is a greater awareness of the role of the mind in healing," she said.

"Illnesses are related to unhappiness in several ways. One is that any kind of distress interferes with the body's immunological system. Further, when we try to satisfy our frustrations with sweets, caffeine, alcohol, etc., we contribute to the deterioration of the body.

"A placebo (often a sugar pill, taken for its psychological effect) seems to work with many people. Why not make use of that feeling? It's your belief system that works. That's where it's at. If you believe you are going to get well, you will — from whatever therapy you use.

"We are too dependent on authority figures in our society to make us well. The important thing to remember is that we have more of an ability to heal ourselves.

"You need to know if the problem is stress-related. Sometimes you don't even realize you're under stress. Illnesses have a multiplicity of causes, certainly. But even when 'something's going around,' sometimes you get it and sometimes you don't."

"If you're the psychosomatic type, and you know a certain part of your body is apt to give you problems, you need to learn how to avoid the problem that might cause you to become sick. Heighten your awareness of your condition. Take care of your mental health, and avoid stress."

How do you heighten your awareness to know when you're under stress?

There are several techniques. One is biofeedback, another is meditation, and a third is psychotherapy. She suggests selecting the method that works best for you.

Berger, who holds a master of social work degree from the Columbia University School of Social Work and has a background of more than 25 years in the field, said there is only a small percentage of medical doctors who believe in holistic healing, although that is changing.

But don't germs cause illness?

Yes, and the body heals itself through its immunological system, she said. But your mental state of mind, including how you feel about being well or ill can hinder or help the process.

Berger said she knows of no one currently practicing Options Therapy in the San Diego area. While here for the winter, she is doing some private counseling through an office in Hillcrest (call 294-9293), and plans to expand that in the fall when she returns to El Cajon to make her home here. This time the move will be permanent.

Figure 41

OBSERVER

Top Heavy

F-A-T.

The word summons up nasty images. Unattractive, unsexy and unhealthy, to name a few. It's a portrait created by a multibillion-dollar industry ballyhooing sauna suits, fat farms, powdered protein, pills, candy, drinks. The message is clear enough: We are undisciplined slobs.

For everyone beyond Hardcore Gimmicks and needing a new or last resort, there is the "Fat Class," the think-thin brainchild of psychologists Marian Hirsch and Linda Pilcher, designed to prune unwanted inches from the bodies of the calorically-inclined even as it modifies their behavior. As unlikely as it always sounds, your weight is all in your head.

Says one rehabilitated food-aholic: "It's mind over mouth." Yet temptation remains only an arm's-length away. And it's when she is downhearted that this 28-year-old art distributor is short on willpower, and seeks refuge in a fistful of Fritos. "It's all in my head. And I finally decided I wanted my outside to look as good as my inside." Gone are the bridge-mix binges and Big Mac attacks. Gone also are 15 pounds. "The class made me realize why I eat, and made me question those eating habits. It helped me with my self-image."

No matter what our body's fat content, many of us consider ourselves grossly overweight—an image that has been nurtured by twentieth-century styles pushing slimness. But therapists Hirsch and Pilcher have waged war against this Thin-Is-In mentality and designed a plan that calls for an end to the obsession with losing weight.

The scheme is discussion. Ten would-be thin people gather once a week at the Meramec Counseling Center for two hours to talk out their frustrations. During the 12-week course, they touch on such food-related topics as the meaning of eating, the connection between eating and feelings, parent-child relationships, assertiveness, body-image and sexuality.

"I like the support and the sharing that comes with being in a class—not tackling this alone," said one woman.

What about exercise? Well, the class is heavy on mental workouts—essay questions, group discussions, relaxation techniques, guided fantasy, role playing and bio-energetics (using the body to act out your feelings). But the program is designed to develop the mind before the muscle. Losing weight is secondary to understanding why you turn to food for comfort. And it is this philosophy that sets the "Fat Class" apart from other weight-loss programs.

"Beginners are not ready to talk about losing weight," explained Linda Pilcher. "They get defensive." Fitness becomes an issue only in the intermediate and advanced classes where diet, nutrition and exercise are discussed. Goals and meal planning are generally developed by the individuals, but the aid of Hirsch and Pilcher can be enlisted.

The two-year-old "Fat Class" emerged while Linda Pilcher was doing research for her dissertation. She is currently working on a doctorate in counseling psychology at Washington University. Her colleague, Marian Hirsch, holds a master's degree in social work. And both have been in private practice for three years.

The classes run $200. But as some people say, that's just about the cost of a three-month supply of diet chocolate drinks.

—Donna Carmon

Figure 42

FLORIDA'S LARGEST WEEKLY NEWSPAPER

OUR 22nd YEAR

Serving Hallandale, Hollywood, Aventura, North Miami Beach & North Dade

Member of Florida Press Assn. and National Newspaper Assn.

HALLANDALE DIGEST

Vol. 21 No. 54   Established 1963   43,000 AUDITED CIRCULATION   44 Pages in 6 Sections

Rational-Emotional Therapy VS Drugs Favored At Med-Stress Center

By Ann Mankowski

Can a woman who has smoked for twenty years quit a habit that has injured her from being in optimum health in one therapy session at Med Stress Center? Yes, it did happen and the following week co-office workers called for appointments seeking help to combat their weight and smoking habits.

Everyone has problems. Problem solving is very important for one's well being.

Dr. Alan Schiaks, a clinical psychologist, has opened Med-Stress Center, located at 4700 Sheridan Street in Hollywood. Med-Stress Centers offer a low-cost treatment program which specializes in panic attacks, weight loss, depression, sexual dysfunctions and other psychological problems brought on by stress. Dr. Schiaks holds a Masters Degrees from Nova University and a Doctorate Degree from the University of Louvain, Belgium.

He just completed a three year study at the University of Southern California Medical School with Dr. Dennis Munjack on Erectile Dysfunction which will be published in the September issue of "Journal of Sex and Marital Therapy." Dr. Schiaks is also an Associate Fellow at the Institute for Rational-Emotive Therapy in New York where he worked with Dr. Albert Ellis, founder of Rational-Emotive Therapy is a brief psychotherapy which zeros in on problems for immediate relief. Fears, phobias, poor marital relationships, sexual dysfunction, smoking and weight loss are only some of the problems that can be cured quickly.

Since Dr. Schiaks covers such a wide range of therapy I asked him to extensify on one major problem that confronts our society now that being alcoholism.

Here are three of the "Twenty Psychological Techniques for Not Drinking" which was written by Dr. A. Schiaks.

Don't put your ego on the line. Anytime you place your ego (yourself) on the line, you are likely to inhibit your chances at successful performance. You should not confuse your worth to yourself with your success or failure at any activity, especially drinking! Criticizing yourself will tend not to motivate you on your road to sobriety, example: "how can a crummy person like me ever change." You may choose to dislike your behavior of drinking and all the obnoxious consequences that go along with it, but disliking yourself will keep you less motivated to change.

Tackle the underlying cause of your "need" to drink more when it occurs. Here we refer to the psychological rather than the biological causes which create so-called needs to grab a drink under stress. When you say you need something, in distinction to wanting it, a necessity is implied. That is, you are asserting that you cannot do without it. Need denotes the inability to do without — we need for example, food and water. Human beings quite frequently define their life situation in terms of needs instead of say hopes and desires (I need a new dress, or I need to be loved). More often than the result of this is that these needs are not fulfilled and when they aren't the person becomes

anxious and tense and begins to rely on various ends of crutches to handle his tensions. For the overeater food is the crutch, for the alcoholic, alcohol. Virtually all of these psychological needs actually are not needs at all but beliefs, ideas, assumptions, or fixed-concepts stated by the individual in terms of, "I must have." The belief that one must have is a socially acquired attitude and it can be unlearned as it was learned. When this belief system is successfully done away with, the underlying tensions it creates are also removed.

Dealing with feelings of inadequacy and worthlessness. Some people drink while others may drink to help them over with feelings of worthlessness and inadequacy resulting from what they tell themselves about how well they are doing (in their job, love life, interpersonal relations, in school, as a parent, etc.) and how they believe they should be doing (rather than how they prefer to be doing). Negatively approaching oneself because of real or presumed rejections and disapproval by others is another major cause of tension and anxiety which leads to drinking in short, fear of failure, which comes from believing that one should be perfectly adequate and competent in all performances, and fear of rejection, which stems from believing that one should be loved and approved of by a virtually everybody, both lead to the irrational belief that one is worthless, inadequate, or no good as a person.

Dr. Schiaks does not

believe in lengthy and expensive therapy sessions but in a short-term program to pinpoint the individual problem and give the patient solutions that will work quickly.

For further information Dr. Schiaks can be reached by calling 962-4777 in Broward or 945-1321 in Dade.

Start today in realizing a better future for yourself. Every day counts!

Figure 43

Finally, when planning a publicity campaign or staging a media event, such as opening a new office, it is often useful to have a **press kit** ready to distribute to media representatives. The press kit should contain samples of any promotional materials you've used, photos of yourself and your practice associates, and copies of previous articles in which you have been featured. In addition, you might include biographies of yourself and your practice associates along with copies of ads you've used to promote your practice (Tellem, 1983). The press kit provides a portfolio of you and your practice that is representative of the image you want projected. It is a pretty standard tool that lends a professional edge to your relations with media and carries a message that you are serious about your publicity efforts. A definitive reference on publicity is *Lesly's Public Relations Handbook* (1983). Now in its third edition this volume can help you to better understand the finer points of working with public relations professionals and journalists so you don't have to simply finesse media relations.

We'd like to conclude this chapter by saying that whatever kind of promotional activities you engage in, you should pay heed to the ethical principles of your professional discipline. If you think there are shortcomings in the standards then work to have them changed. There are important lessons to be learned from the experiences of other professions who let the decisions be made by the courts. We are reprinting those portions of the various mental health disciplines' ethical standards that are concerned with advertising and public statements in the appendix. Take a few minutes to look them over.

CHAPTER SUMMARY

Promotional tools are the vehicles that carry your marketing plans into action. Their carefully devised application can bring success; careless use can spell disaster.

An essential skill for the therapist to hone is copywriting. It's unnecessary to think of writing copy as requiring great creativity. Instead, it's better to think clearly about your intended audience and how to communicate with them in a simple and straightforward manner. A common sense approach is a good starting point.

The variety of promotional materials therapists have been using demonstrate the wide range of ideas that can be effective. Remember that different segments and different markets may not respond to the same content and appeal. For that reason it is essential to fully understand your target segment and your market. To minimize unnecessary expense and aggravation it's wise to test the effectiveness of any promotional materials. Irrespective of the tools and techniques you choose, we advocate remaining within the confines of professional ethical standards.

REFERENCES

Baum, L. (1984), Lawyers' ads attract working class clients. *Miami Herald.* (3/26/84).

Benn, A. (1978), *The 27 most common mistakes in advertising.* New York: AMACOM, American Management Association.

Bloom, P. N. (1984), Effective marketing for professional services. *Harvard Business Review, 62,* 102-110.

Caples, J. (1974), *Tested advertising methods.* 4th edition. Englewood Cliffs, NJ: Prentice-Hall.

Lesly, P. (Ed.) (1983), *Lesly's public relations handbook.* Englewood Cliffs, NJ: Prentice-Hall.

Ogilvy, D. (1982), *Ogilvy on advertising.* New York: Crown.

Tellem, S. M. (1983), Building a new or better image for your practice through solid media relations. *Health Marketing Quarterly, 1* (1), 41-47.

CHAPTER 7

EPILOGUE

BY FIRST recognizing that problems to be solved in establishing, expanding, or redirecting a psychotherapy practice involve the same kinds of solutions that are used by people in virtually any other business setting you become ready to function as a business manager. To be successful, and we sincerely hope you are, you must acquire an alphabet of managerial skills that may be assembled in a myriad of ways. Many of these skills are relatively easy to develop through observation and experience, or like accounting can be purchased when needed. We believe that far and away the single most important set of understandings for effective practice management are those contained in the discipline of marketing. It should now be evident that marketing concepts can be readily understood and adapted to the multi-faceted practice problems faced by psychotherapists. Since marketing is not just a set of tasks, but encompasses a modification of management style, marketing should become a central theme in your practice philosophy, so you are a practitioner of integrated marketing.

In summary, marketing is a two-way communication between therapists and clients and its use enhances the relationship benefits to both. As far as individual therapists are concerned there is more than ample justification for upgrading marketing efforts. Use of marketing tools allows us to pursue the very activities, conducting psychotherapy, that initially attracted us to the profession. By incorporating a data-based approach to planning and modifying the marketing mix we can maximize control over our practice. Greater control cannot guarantee that we will have exactly the kind of practice we'd like, but it increases the odds. Marketing also aids in eliciting referrals of those clients we can best help by virtue of increased information about the qualifications and specializations of therapists being available to clients and referral agents. Hence, marketing can assist in promoting better services and increased consumer satisfaction.

The benefits are greater reaching however, since a marketing orientation advocates educating the general public about psychotherapy and thereby promotes public welfare. Consumers become more knowledgeable about the services offered by therapists through marketing. As a result, psychotherapists, the services we provide, and those who receive these services gain increased acceptance. Marketing also stimulates demand. While greater demand may be helpful to individual therapists it is also good for consumers because more demand leads to more competition, which may ultimately result in the highest quality services at the lowest possible cost.

We've included examples of how the various marketing tools have been used by therapists. Often therapists have used them intuitively; others were studied and planned to achieve a specific result. Since therapists began practicing privately, most marketing activities have fallen within the categories we've termed passive and intentional. We predict the future holds major changes in practice patterns, reimbursement policies, types of services offered, and sources of referrals. There is going to be a continuing growth of the private practice sector of mental health services providers as long as there is a demand for the services and there are training programs to prepare therapists. As a consequence the market will be extremely competitive. To take advantage of new opportunities, like the viability of "new" segments, therapists must become more systematic in our marketing efforts. We hope the preceding chapters have given you a sufficient foundation of marketing principles that you can build on so you are able to succeed in the increasingly competitive and changing environment.

Some therapists view marketing activities as an investment. From this vantage point therapists can calculate return-on-investment ratios. For others, their outlays are thought of as practice overhead. Either way, the cost for marketing are both tax deductible and legitimate expenses.

The application of marketing principles to the psychotherapy practice is on a frontier. The 1980s have already witnessed a host of challenges to traditional forms of professional practice. Employee Assistance Programs, for instance, have significantly altered the ways in which many of us now practice. Although it was beyond the scope of this book to address the details of EAPs, it is worth noting that they represent an avenue for practice enhancement. There are many ways to learn more about EAPs such as reading *EAP Digest* (2145 Crooks Rd., Suite 103,

Troy, MI 48084). However, the marketing process we've described in earlier chapters will be of use in this content-specific area. Similarly, we can think of a marketing driven approach to working with third party payers. This was done by the American Psychiatric Association whose marketing consultant conducted an educational program to promote increased mental health benefits in insurance coverage (1985).

We anticipate many developments in the near future and expect that a vast number of new techniques will be developed that you can readily integrate into your practice. There are most likely to come from practitioners who've adapted their thinking and management style to include a marketing orientation. These advances will go hand-in-hand with new developments in empirical research emanating from academic settings. Presumably, academicians and practitioners can become partners in finding behavioral science solutions to significant practice problems.

REFERENCES

Herrington, B. S. (1985), Marketing consultant to APA reports progress to assembly. *Psychiatric News, 20* (23), 1, 12.

APPENDIX A

PSYCHOTHERAPY PRACTICE PLANNING FORM

I. Mission Statement

A. My purpose for conducting my practice is

_____

_____

B. The services I offer are

____ short-term therapy	____ agency consultation
____ long-term therapy	to _____
____ individual therapy	_____
____ MFT	
____ group therapy	
____ Education to	____ Assessment/Evaluation
____ professionals	____ personality
____ students	____ psychoeducational
____ public workshops	____ vocational
____ clinical supervision	____ forensic/competency
____ other	____ custody
	____ employment
	____ other

Populations Served

____ children	Public service (e.g.,
____ adolescents	serving on boards)
____ adults	_____
____ geriatrics	_____
____ other	_____

II. Resources

A. Facilities

1. What office space, equipment, and materials are required to provide the services stated in I.B.?_____

_____

_____

2. Are these presently available?

   YES (GO TO II. B.)   NO

3. What is needed?_____

   _____

4. How will they be obtained?_____

   _____

B. Finances (determine on annual basis)

   1. How much does it cost per month for the facilities required to conduct your desired practice?

      a. rent $ _____
      b. utilities $ _____
      c. phone $ _____
      d. furnishings (own/rental) $ _____
      e. insurance $ _____
      f. salaries $ _____
      g. professional materials $ _____
      h. offices supplies $ _____
      i. miscellaneous $ _____
                MONTHLY TOTAL = $ _____

   2. How much money is available to spend on your practice?

      a. $ _____ per month
      b. $ _____ from practice income
      c. $ _____ from other income
      d. $ _____ from loans, gifts, etc.

   3. Are these sufficient funds available each month to meet expenses?

      YES (GO TO II. C.)   NO

      How will they be obtained?_____

      _____

C. Expertise

   1. What specific skills are needed to provide the services identified in I.B.? _____

      _____

   2. The skills I will work on are _____

      _____

   3. Plans for skill development

      a. I will **maintain** my skills by _____

         _____

      b. I will **up-grade** my skills by _____

      _____

      c. I will **expand** my skills by _____

      _____

  D. Referral sources
    1. How are clients referred and by whom?
    2. What other referral sources are available?
    3. From which ones do you wish to increase your referrals?
    4. What specific plans do you have for increasing them?

III. Practice Objectives

  A. Long-term goals (e.g., 3-5 years)
    1. Financial: _____

    _____

    2. Facilities: _____

    _____

    3. Employees: _____

    _____

    4. Expansion: _____

    _____

    5. Other: _____

    _____

  B. Short-term Goals (within 18 months)
    1. Financial: _____
    2. Facilities: _____
    3. Employees: _____
    4. Expansion: _____
    5. Other: _____

IV. Professional Career Objectives

  A. Long-term (3-5 years)

  B. Short-term (< 18 months)

V. Evaluation — Strategy for continual evaluation of practice goals and objectives and procedures for revising plans.

  1. What data will be considered? _____

  _____

  2. What criteria will be used to assess if goals/objectives were met?

  _____

APPENDIX B

PSYCHOTHERAPY PRACTICE MARKETING PLANNING FORM

I. Mission Statement

    A. My purpose for conducting my practice is _____
_____

    B. The services I offer are _____
_____

II. Situation Analysis

    A. What are the segments that exist in my market and what is their approximate number?

       1. _____ (N=   )
       2. _____ (N=   )
       3. _____ (N=   )
       4. _____ (N=   )

    B. How are these segments currently being served by the competition?_____

       1. How many other therapists are there? (categorize by discipline) _____

       2. What agencies represent competition? _____

       3. What is the fee structure among the competition? _____
_____

       4. What is your position relative to the competition? _____
_____

    C. Current practice characteristics

       1. Number of clients seen per month is _____
       2. Types of clients treated are _____
       3. Fee structure range: $ ____ to $ ____; average: $ ____
       4. Collection rate: _____ %
       5. Clients using third party payers: _____ %
       6. Third party payment sources: _____
       7. Referral sources
          a. _____ client referred
          b. _____ professional referred
              by whom, specifically? _____
       8. Other resources available to me are _____

    D. Life cycle analysis

       1. practice: _____

       2. therapist: _____

       3. favored therapeutic modalities: _____

III. Trend Analysis

    A. What social trends have I noticed over the recent past?

      _____

    B. What do I think will come into vogue during the next 6 to 12 months? _____

    C. What developments have been occurring in my community?

      _____

    D. What must I do to prepare for these trends? _____

      _____

IV. Problems and Opportunities

    A. What difficulties might arise which could negatively affect my practice? _____

    B. What if _____?

      I would _____

    C. What appears to be happening that I could capitalize on? __

      _____

    D. What changes in third party payment reimbursement and regulations affecting psychotherapy are likely?_____

      _____

V. Marketing Objectives

    A. To which clients do I want to increase services and by how much? _____

    B. To which group will I decrease services and by how much?_

      _____

    C. What new segments will I target?_____

      _____

       1. What services will I offer each? _____

       2. How much service will I offer to each newly targeted segment? _____

       3. Describe each new segment as specifically as possible according to number that exist, geographic area where located, proximity to practice location, demographic characteristics, psychographic features, and possible promotional tools to reach them.

VI. Marketing Strategy for Each Segment

   A. Marketing mix

      1. Service features: _____

      2. Promotional tools

         a. sales promotion: _____

         b. personal sales: _____

         c. advertising: _____

         d. publicity: _____

   B. What are the goals for your message? (educate, persuade, change attitude, etc.) _____

   C. What is the best medium to reach your selected segment with this message? _____

   D. What strategy or strategies will be most effective? _____
_____

   E. What is your message? _____

VII. Resource Allocation

   A. Who will be responsible for which elements of the marketing plan? _____

   B. How much time will be spent per month? _____

   C. What is the budget allocated to implement the plan? $ ____

VIII. Control and Review

   A. How will I know my efforts have been successful?_____
_____

   B. How frequently will the plan be monitored? _____

   C. How and when will I revise my overall plan? _____
_____

APPENDIX C

AACD ETHICAL STANDARDS RELEVANT
TO MARKETING

Section F: Private Practice

2. In advertising services as a private practitioner, the member must advertise the services in such a manner so as to accurately inform the public as to services, expertise, profession, and techniques of counseling in a professional manner. A member who assumes an executive leadership role in the organization shall not permit his/her name to be used in professional notices during periods when not actively engaged in the private practice counseling.

   The member may list the following: highest relevant degree, type and level of certification or license, type and/or description of services, and other relevant information. Such information must not contain false, inaccurate, misleading, partial, out-of-context, or deceptive material or standards.

Excerpt from the *Ethical Standards* of the American Association for Counseling and Development, Alexandria, VA. Used by permission.

APPENDIX D

AAMFT ETHICAL PRINCIPLES RELEVANT TO MARKETING

Advertising

Marriage and family therapists engage in appropriate informational activities, including those that enable laypersons to choose marriage and family services on an informed basis.

7.1 Marriage and family therapists accurately represent their competence, education, training, and experience relevant to their practice of marriage and family therapy.

7.2 Marriage and family therapists claim as evidence of educational qualifications only those degrees (a) from regionally-accredited institutions or (b) from institutions accredited by states which license or certify marriage and family therapists, but only if such regulation is recognized by AAMFT.

7.3 Marriage and family therapists assure that advertisements and publications, whether in directories, announcement cards, newspapers, or on radio or television, are formulated to convey information that is necessary for the public to make an appropriate selection. Information could include:

1. office information, such as name, address, telephone number, credit card acceptability, fee structure, languages spoken, and office hours;

2. appropriate degrees, state licensure and/or certification, and AAMFT Clinical Member status; and

3. description of practice.

7.4 Marriage and family therapists do not use a name which could mislead the public concerning the identity, responsibility, source, and status of those practicing under that name and do not hold themselves out as being partners or associates of a firm if they are not.

7.5 Marriage and family therapists do not use any professional identification (such as a professional card, office sign, letterhead, or telephone or association directory listing), if it includes a statement or claim that is false, fraudulent, misleading or deceptive. A statement is false, fraudulent, misleading, or deceptive if it (a) contains a material misrepresentation of fact; (b) fails to state any material fact necessary to make the statement, in light of all circumstances, not misleading; or (c) is intended to or is likely to create an unjustified expectation.

7.6   Marriage and family therapists correct, wherever possible, false, misleading, or inaccurate information and representations made by others concerning the marriage and family therapist's qualifications, services or products.

7.7   Marriage and family therapists make certain that the qualifications of persons in their employ are represented in a manner that is not false, misleading, or deceptive.

7.8   Marriage and family therapists may represent themselves as specializing within a limited area of marriage and family therapy, but may not hold themselves out as specialists without being able to provide evidence of training, education, and supervised experience in settings which meet recognized professional standards.

7.9   Marriage and family therapist Clinical Members — not associates, students or organizations — may identify their membership in AAMFT in public information or advertising materials.

7.10   Marriage and family therapists may not use the initials AAMFT following their name in the manner of an academic degree.

7.11   Marriage and family therapists may not use the AAMFT logo. The Association (which is the sole owner of its name, logo, and the abbreviated initials AAMFT) and its committees and regional divisions, operating as such, may use the logo. A regional division of AAMFT may use the AAMFT insignia to list its individual members as a group (e.g., in the Yellow Pages), when all Clinical Members practicing within a directory district have been invited to list themselves in the directory, any one or more members may do so.

7.12   Marriage and family therapists use their membership in AAFMT only in connection with their clinical and professional activities.

Excerpt from *AAMFT Code of Ethical Principles for Marriage and Family Therapists.* American Association for Marriage and Family Therapy, Washington, D.C. Used by permission.

APPENDIX E

AMERICAN PSYCHOLOGICAL ASSOCIATION ETHICAL PRINCIPLES RELEVANT TO MARKETING

Principle 4: Public Statements

Public statements, announcements of services, advertising, and promotional activities of psychologists serve the purpose of helping the public make informed judgments and choices. Psychologists represent accurately and objectively their professional qualifications, affiliations, and functions, as well as those of the institutions or organizations with which they or the statements may be associated. In public statements providing psychological information or professional opinions or providing information about the availability of psychological products, publications, and services, psychologists base their statements on scientifically acceptable psychological findings and techniques with full recognition of the limits and uncertainties of such evidence.

a. When accouncing or advertising professional services, psychologists may list the following information to describe the provider and services provided: name, highest relevant academic degree earned from a regionally accredited institution, date, type, and level of certification or licensure, diplomate status, APA membership status, address, telepone number, office hours, a brief listing of the type of psychological services offered, an appropriate presentation of fee information, foreign languages spoken, and policy with regard to third-party payments. Additional relevant or important consumer information may be included if not prohibited by other sections of these Ethical Principles.

b. In announcing or advertising the availability of psychological products, publications, or services, psychologists do not present their affiliation with any organization in a manner that falsely implies sponsorship or certification by that organization. In particular and for example, psychologists do not state APA membership or fellow status in a way to suggest that such status implies specialized professional competence or qualifications. Public statements include, but are not limited to, communication by means of periodical, book, list, directory, television, radio, or motion picture. They do not contain (i) a

175

false, fraudulent, misleading, deceptive, or unfair statement; (ii) a misinterpretation of fact or a statement likely to mislead or deceive because in context it makes only a partial disclosure of relevant facts; (iii) a testimonial from a patient regarding the quality of a psychologist's services or products; (iv) a statement intended or likely to create false or unjustified expectations of favorable results; (v) a statement implying unusual, unique, or one-of-a-kind abilities; (vi) a statement intended or likely to appeal to a client's fears, anxieties, or emotions concerning the possible results of failure to obtain the offered services; (vii) a statement concerning the comparative desirability of offered services; (viii) a statement of direct solicitation of individual clients.

c. Psychologists do not compensate or give anything of value to a representative of the press, radio, television, or other communication medium in anticipation of or in return for professional publicity in a news item. A paid advertisement must be identified as such, unless it is apparent from the context that it is a paid advertisement. If communicated to the public by use of radio or television, an advertisement is prerecorded and approved for broadcast by the psychologist, and a recording of the actual transmission is retained by the psychologist.

d. Announcements or advertisements of "personal growth groups," clinics, and agencies give a clear statement of purpose and a clear description of the experiences to be provided. The education, training, and experience of the staff members are appropriately specified.

e. Psychologists associated with the development or promotion of psychological devices, books, or other products offered for commercial sale make reasonable efforts to ensure that announcements and advertisements are presented in a professional, scientifically acceptable, and factually informative manner.

f. Psychologists do not participate for personal gain in commercial announcements or advertisements recommending to the public the purchase or use of proprietary or single-source products or services when that participation is based solely upon their identification as psychologists.

g. Psychologists present the science of psychology and offer their services, products, and publications fairly and accurately, avoiding misrepresentation through sensationalism, exaggeration, or superficiality. Psychologists are guided by the primary obligation to aid the public in developing informed judgments, opinions, and choices.

h. As teachers, psychologists ensure that statements in catalogs and course outlines are accurate and not misleading, particularly in terms of subject matter to be covered, bases for evaluating progress, and the nature of course experiences. Announcements, brochures, or advertisements describing workshops, seminars, or other educational programs accurately describe the audience for which the program is intended as well as eligibility requirements, educational objectives, and nature of the materials to be covered. These announcements also accurately represent the education, training, and experience of the psychologists presenting the programs and any fees involved.

i. Public announcements or advertisements soliciting research participants in which clinical services or other professional services are offered as an inducement make clear the nature of the services as well as the costs and other obligations to be accepted by participants in the research.

j. A psychologist accepts the obligation to correct others who represent the psychologist's professional qualifications, or associations with products or services, in a manner incompatible with these guidelines.

k. Individual diagnostic and therapeutic services are provided only in the context of a professional psychological relationship. When personal advice is given by means of public lectures or demonstrations, newspaper or magazine articles, radio or television programs, mail, or similar media, the psychologist utilizes the most curernt relevant data and exercises the highest level of professional judgment.

l. Products that are described or presented by means of public lectures or demonstrations, newspaper or magazine articles, radio or television programs, or similar media meet the same recognized standards as exists for products used in the context of a professional relationship.

Excerpt from *Ethical Principles of Psychologists.* American Psychological Association, Washington, D.C. Used by permission.

APPENDIX F

AMHCA ETHICAL PRINCIPLES RELEVANT TO MARKETING

Principle 4: Public Statements

Clinical mental health counselors in their professional roles may be expected or required to make public statements providing counseling information, professional opinions, or supply information about the availability of counseling products and services. In making such statements, clinical mental health counselors take full account of the limits and uncertainties of present counseling knowledge and techniques. They represent, as objectively as possible, their professional qualifications, affiliations, and functions, as well as those of the institutions or organizations with which the statements may be associated. All public statements, announcements of services, and promotional activities should serve the purpose of providing sufficient information to aid the consumer public in making informed judgments and choices on matters that concern it.

a. When announcing professional services, clinical mental health counselors limit the information to: name, highest relevant degree conferred, certification or licensure, address, telephone number, office hours, cost of services, and a brief explanation of the types of services offered but not evaluative as to their quality of uniqueness. They will no contain testimonials by implication. They will not claim uniqueness of skill or methods beyond those available to others in the profession unless determined by acceptable and public scientific evidence.

b. In announcing the availability of counseling services or products, clinical mental health counselors will not display their affiliations with organizations or agencies in a manner that implies the sponsorship or certification of the organization or agency. They will not name their employer or professional associations unless the services are in fact to be provided by or under the responsible, direct supervision and continuing control of such organizations or agencies.

c. Clinical mental health counselors associated with the development or promotion of counseling device, books, or other products offered for commercial sale will make every effort to insure that announcements and advertisement are presented in a professional and factually informative manner without unsupported claims of superiority; [all infor-

179

mation] must be supported by scientifically acceptable evidence or by willingness to aid and encourage independent professional scrutiny of scientific test.

d. Clinical mental health counselors engaged in radio, television or other public media activities will no participate in commercial announcements recommending to the general public the purchase or use of any proprietary or single-source product or service.

e. Clinical mental health counselors who describe counseling or the services of professional counselors to the general public accept the obligation to present the material fairly and accurately, avoiding misrepresentation through sensationalism, exaggeration or superficiality. Clinical mental health counselors will be guided by the primary obligation to aid the public in forming their own informed judgments, opinions and choices.

f. As teachers, clinical mental health counselors ensure that statements in catalogs and course outlines are accurate, particularly in terms of subject matter to be covered, bases for grading, and nature of classroom experiences. As practitioners providing private services, CMH counselors avoid improper, direct solicitation of clients and the conflict of interest inherent therein.

g. Clinical mental health counselors accept the obligation to correct others who may represent their professional qualifications or associations with products or services in a manner incompatible with these guidelines.

INDEX